Foreign Direct Investment in the United States: Benefits, Suspicions, and Risks with Special Attention to FDI from China

Theodore H. Moran and Lindsay Oldenski

PETERSON INSTITUTE FOR INTERNATIONAL ECONOMICS
Washington, DC
August 2013

MIX
Paper from
responsible sources
FSC www.fsc.org FSC® C010236

Theodore H. Moran, nonresident senior fellow, has been associated with the Peterson Institute for International Economics since 1998. He holds the Marcus Wallenberg Chair at the School of Foreign Service in Georgetown University. He is the founder of the Landegger Program in International Business Diplomacy at the university and serves as director there. He also serves as a member of Huawei's International Advisory Council. Since 2007 he has served as associate to the US National Intelligence Council on international business issues. Moran has published numerous books on foreign direct investment, including *Outward Foreign Direct Investment and US Exports, Jobs, and R&D: Implications for US Policy* (2013), *Foreign Direct Investment and Development: Launching a Second Generation of Policy Research: Avoiding the Mistakes of the First, Reevaluating Policies for Developed and Developing Countries* (2011), *China's Strategy to Secure Natural Resources: Risks, Dangers, and Opportunities* (2010), *Three Threats: An Analytical Framework for the CFIUS Process* (2009), *Harnessing Foreign Direct Investment for Development: Policies for Developed and Developing Countries* (2006), and *Does Foreign Direct Investment Promote Development?* (coedited with Magnus Blomstrom and Edward Graham, 2005).

Lindsay Oldenski is assistant professor in the Landegger Program in International Business Diplomacy at Georgetown University's School of Foreign Service. Prior to joining the Georgetown faculty, she taught at the Johns Hopkins University School of Advanced International Studies and California State University, San Marcos. She was also an economist at the US Department of Treasury, an analyst at the Federal Reserve Bank of Boston, and a consultant in the biotech industry. Her research on international trade and multinational organizations has been published in both academic journals and policy forums. She received her PhD in economics from the University of California, San Diego, and her Master in Public Policy from the Harvard University Kennedy School of Government. She is coauthor of *Outward Foreign Direct Investment and US Exports, Jobs, and R&D: Implications for US Policy* (2013).

PETERSON INSTITUTE FOR INTERNATIONAL ECONOMICS
1750 Massachusetts Avenue, NW
Washington, DC 20036-1903
(202) 328-9000   FAX: (202) 659-3225
www.piie.com

Adam S. Posen, *President*
Edward A. Tureen, *Director of Publications, Marketing, and Web Development*

Typesetting by diacriTech
Printing by United Book Press, Inc.

Printed in the United States of America
15   14   13   5   4   3   2   1

Library of Congress Cataloging-in-Publication Data
Moran, Theodore H., 1943–
   Foreign direct investment in the United States: benefits, suspicions, and risks with special attention to FDI from China / Theodore H. Moran.
      pages cm
   Includes bibliographical references.
   ISBN 978-0-88132-660-4
   1. Investments, Chinese—United States.
2. Investments, Foreign—China.   3. United States—Economic policy—2009–   I. Title.
   HG4910.M664 2013
   332.67'351073—dc23

                                    2012048602

This publication has been subjected to a prepublication peer review intended to ensure analytical quality. The views expressed are those of the authors. This publication is part of the overall program of the Peterson Institute for International Economics, as endorsed by its Board of Directors, but it does not necessarily reflect the views of individual members of the Board or of the Institute's staff or management. The Institute is an independent, private, nonprofit institution for rigorous, intellectually honest study and open discussion of international economic policy. Its work is made possible by financial support from a highly diverse group of philanthropic foundations, private corporations, and interested individuals, as well as by income on its capital fund. For a list of Institute supporters, please see www.piie.com/supporters.cfm.

Contents

Boxes

Preface

Foreign direct investment (FDI) has emerged as a central force in expanding global economic activity in recent decades. Much of the public's attention has focused on US-based multinational corporations (MNCs) whose foreign affiliates produce goods and services in volumes that are twice as large as total world exports. Less well appreciated, perhaps, the United States has been and still is the largest host to inward FDI in the world, receiving more than twice as much direct investment as China, which ranked second in 2010.

These foreign investments have provided enormous benefits to the United States, but they are not without controversy. Among other things, Americans worry about whether foreign investment jeopardizes US independence, especially in the industries related to national security and energy. A public debate over Chinese and Persian Gulf investments a few years ago, for example, replayed concerns voiced in the 1980s in the United States when Japan bought such high-profile US assets as Pebble Beach golf courses and Rockefeller Center.

The purpose of this study is to examine the impact of FDI in the United States, including its effects on jobs, wages, productivity, research and development (R&D), and trade itself. The work looks at different sectors in services and manufacturing and specifically studies the impact of Chinese investment compared with investment in the United States by other countries. A major part of this inquiry is an examination of the national security issues raised by investment in sensitive sectors, including energy and telecommunications, by Chinese and other foreign investors. Beyond the obvious difference in systems, Chinese FDI is a particular concern because of tensions between Washington and Beijing over espionage and allegations of cyberwarfare.

As always with studies by the Peterson Institute for International Economics, this study is intended to establish the facts and analyze their implications as objectively as possible, without serving any particular interests or ideological agenda. It is our hope to clear the air about foreign and specifically Chinese investment in the United States by supplying an unbiased analytical basis on which public policy decisions can be debated and made. The authors are Theodore H. Moran, nonresident senior fellow at the Peterson Institute and holder of the Marcus Wallenberg Chair at the School of Foreign Service in Georgetown University and, Lindsay Oldenski, assistant professor of economics at Georgetown University. Moran also serves as a member of the International Advisory Council of the Chinese electronics multinational Huawei. The work of these authors follows in an important line of earlier Institute research by Edward M. Graham, Paul Krugman, David Marchick, and Moran himself. Indeed Moran, Thomas Horst, and C. Fred Bergsten launched this field of inquiry in the late 1970s.

Moran and Oldenski's starting point is to document the sheer magnitude of FDI in the United States. FDI flows into the United States greatly exceeded FDI flows into China for all years for which data are available.[1] The most recent figures from 2010 show that outward flows of FDI from the United States were also higher than those of any other country, more than three times as large as FDI flows from the second largest source country, Germany. Within the FDI arena, US multinationals have a dominant presence. The impact of outward investment by American multinationals in the home US economy is the focus of a companion volume to this study.[2]

The authors' analyses of the impact of FDI on US jobs, productivity, trade, and on the practices of other firms, as well as the national security implications of that FDI flow for the United States, are divided into five chapters.

Chapter 1 reviews concerns that originated with Japanese investment in the United States in the 1980s and updates comparisons of the wages paid, value-added, total factor productivity, imports, exports, and R&D of companies owned by foreign investors—including by Chinese investors but also by the overwhelmingly more substantial inward FDI from countries in the Organization for Economic Cooperation and Development (OECD)—with those attributes of comparable US firms (US MNCs and US non-MNCs).

Chapter 2 assesses the motivations for, and costs and benefits from, international investment to a host economy like the United States. Focusing on multinational FDI primarily in manufacturing and services (as opposed to the distinctive dynamics of FDI in the extractive sector, infrastructure, or agribusiness), the authors offer a new synthesis of academic theories of multinational corporate investment. They argue that FDI represents transfers of technology, management, quality control, and marketing know-how across borders that are much more intimate and potent than arm's-length commercial transactions and portfolio investments in which neither side is an affiliate of the

---

1. Except in 2003, when the United States received $53.1 billion and China received $53.5 billion of direct investment.

2. Gary Hufbauer, Theodore Moran, and Lindsay Oldenski, *Outward Foreign Direct Investment and US Exports, Jobs, and R&D: Implications for US Policy.* Policy Analyses in International Economics 101. Washington: Peterson Institute for International Economics, 2013.

other. In this light, FDI offers the potential for horizontal (within industry) and vertical (within company) benefits, and the chapter offers rigorous new calculations of the spillovers of technology and other knowledge to rivals in the US market and of the potentially deliberate transfer of technology and other knowledge to suppliers in the US market—transfers that both raise the total factor productivity of business activity in the United States.

Chapter 3 turns to the relatively new phenomenon of FDI from China in the United States. It examines what the data say about the performance of Chinese investors in terms of employment, wages, exports, imports, R&D, and value added in comparison to other foreign investors from OECD economies, Brazil, Russia, and India. Contrary to fears about potential negative consequences of Chinese FDI, this chapter presents evidence that Chinese firms create a disproportionally high number of high-paying jobs in the United States and that they sometimes even export more from their US locations than they import. New empirical evidence is also presented on the extent to which FDI inflows from all emerging-market economies (including China) result in positive effects on the US economy similar to those from OECD countries. Finally, the chapter examines whether levels of Chinese FDI are high or low relative to what a standard list of factors would lead us to expect and therefore what would be the most likely size of future inflows to the United States from China.

Chapter 4 turns to thorny questions about inward FDI—especially inward FDI via acquisition of existing US firms—and potential national security threats to the United States. Concerns have been forcefully raised by some US lawmakers and officials in this regard. Building on prior Institute work by Graham, Marchick, and Moran, the authors offer a framework to separate plausible national security threats from concerns and worries that are not credible. This threat assessment tool is applied to a few high-profile recently proposed Chinese acquisitions. The threat assessment framework is then generalized into a structure that can be adopted by all OECD countries—indeed by all countries including China—to separate real from implausible national security threats on a rational and consistent basis.

Chapter 5 draws implications for US policies that would enhance the advantages and help avoid missing out on the benefits from inward FDI into the United States.

Like all Peterson Institute books, this work was subject to independent review by external experts. As mentioned above, Moran serves as a member of the International Advisory Council of the Chinese electronics multinational Huawei. Taking this into account, the Peterson Institute took special precautions in peer review to protect against possible bias in the analysis.

The Peterson Institute for International Economics is a private, nonprofit, nonpartisan institution for rigorous, intellectually open, and honest study and discussion of international economic policy. Its purpose is to identify and analyze important issues to making globalization beneficial and sustainable for the people of the United States and the world and then to develop and communicate practical new approaches for dealing with them.

The Institute's work is funded by a highly diverse group of philanthropic foundations, private corporations, and interested individuals, as well as income on its capital fund. About 35 percent of the Institute's resources in our latest fiscal year were provided by contributors from outside the United States. The GE Foundation provided generous support for this study.

The Executive Committee of the Institute's Board of Directors bears overall responsibility for the Institute's direction, gives general guidance and approval to its research program, and evaluates its performance in pursuit of its mission. The Institute's President is responsible for the identification of topics that are likely to become important over the medium term (one to three years) and that should be addressed by Institute scholars. This rolling agenda is set in close consultation with the Institute's research staff, Board of Directors, as well as other stakeholders.

The President makes the final decision to publish any individual Institute study, following independent internal and external review of the work.

The Institute hopes that its research and other activities will contribute to building a stronger foundation for international economic policy around the world. We invite readers of these publications to let us know how they think we can best accomplish this objective.

ADAM S. POSEN, President
August 2013

Authors' Note

The statistical analysis of firm-level data on US multinational companies used in this study was conducted at the Bureau of Economic Analysis (BEA), US Department of Commerce, under arrangements that maintain legal confidentiality requirements. The views expressed are ours and do not reflect official positions of the US Department of Commerce. We thank William Zeile for assistance with the BEA data.

THEODORE H. MORAN
LINDSAY OLDENSKI

Economic Effect of Inward FDI on the United States: Old Apprehensions, New Evidence

Americans have long been ambivalent toward foreign direct investment (FDI) in the United States. Foreign multinational corporations may be a source of capital, technology, and jobs. But what are the implications for US workers as the United States remains the most popular destination for foreign multinational investment, usually through acquisition of existing US firms? Does it matter when a Russian oligarch acquires American steel plants, or when an Indian billionaire becomes the largest single supplier of flat-rolled carbon steel in the United States—a product widely used in defense industries? Are Chinese electronics firms threatening to penetrate US telecommunications networks, conducting surveillance and espionage? Should certain sectors, such as energy or infrastructure, be exempted from foreign ownership or control? What about American industries considered vital to the functioning of the US economy?

Today's concerns about foreign acquisitions and domination of key US industries are not new. The 1980s were full of apprehension that the movement of Japanese companies into the United States could turn the country into a satellite production facility, siphoning off technology to the headquarters market and keeping good jobs and high value-added activities there, while relegating less-good jobs and lower value-added activities to the United States. Then, as now, there were concerns that foreign acquisitions of US semiconductor producers and other high-technology companies might pose a national security threat to the United States. Now, as then, these concerns may be greater than they need to be, at the expense of tangible benefits to the United States.

This chapter begins with a reminder of the largest foreign investors in the United States: Switzerland, the United Kingdom, Japan, Germany, France, the Netherlands, and Canada. Chinese FDI, at least so far, is very small by comparison. This sets the stage for a systematic comparison of how foreign investor performance and behavior compares with those of similar US firms. How do wages, productivity, value added, and research and development (R&D) at the plants of foreign investors match up with those of their US counterparts? How have sales, value added, employment, wages, and R&D spending of foreign multinationals behaved over time, in periods of weak and strong economic activity? Might there be a long-term weakening in the contribution of foreign investors to the US job base, worker earnings, or R&D effort?

FDI is replacing trade as the principal provider of goods and services across borders. In examining what motivates it—a relatively new focus of systematic investigation—chapter 2 identifies the channels through which inward FDI might benefit the US host economy and measures how large such effects could be. Chapter 3 then focuses on US foreign investment from the BRIC countries (Brazil, Russia, India, and China), with special emphasis on inward investment from Chinese firms to the United States, now and in the not-so-distant future. Chapter 4 provides a framework to identify when foreign acquisitions might pose a genuine national security threat and when apprehensions about national security are simply not credible. Chapter 5 draws implications about how to make the United States more attractive as a base for international investment.

Which Countries Engage in FDI?

Before digging into the details of how multinational investors perform when they invest in the United States, it is useful to look first at which countries are actually doing most of the FDI around the world. Figure 1.1 shows the 20 largest home-country exporters of FDI and host-country recipients of FDI flows in 2010. The United States is both the largest source and the largest destination country, and on net US firms do more investing in other countries than other countries do in the United States. China is the fifth largest outward investor, with flows roughly 20 percent of those of the United States in 2010.

Figure 1.1 measures FDI using the flows of foreign capital invested in corporations, as reported by each country and compiled by the United Nations Conference on Trade and Development.[1] These data have the advantage of being widely available for a large number of countries, though there are some drawbacks to using them. They measure the value only of a parent firm's financial stake in an entity and do not capture the economic activity of affiliates. The information may mask idiosyncratic differences in the way each country defines and measures FDI. The numbers also primarily use balance of payments data, which are based on the immediate source of the investment, not the ultimate owner of the multinational doing the investing: The investment may be reported as coming from, say, Luxembourg if that is the most immediate channel through which the capital flowed, but the actual owner of the firm doing the investing could be based in a different country. This is

---

1. See UnctadSTAT database, http://unctadstat.unctad.org.

Figure 1.1 FDI flows by country, 2010

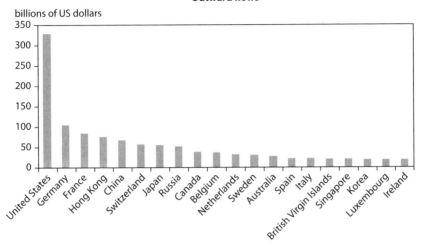

Outward flows

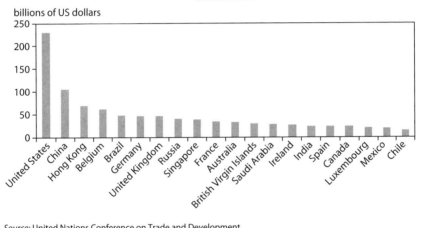

Inward flows

Source: United Nations Conference on Trade and Development.

of particular concern for data from Hong Kong, which is an intermediate stop for many investments going into and coming out of China.[2] Note also that Taiwan is not included as a separate country. To address some of these issues, the US Bureau of Economic Analysis (BEA) also publishes measures of inward FDI constructed using the value added of foreign firms in the United States, a measure that captures the economic activity of firms rather than capital flows alone. The BEA also identifies the source of these direct investments based on the concept of the ultimate beneficial owner (UBO), defined as "that person,

---

2. For a more in-depth discussion of the various types and definitions of FDI flows, see Lipsey (2001).

proceeding up a US affiliate's ownership chain, beginning with and including the foreign parent, that is not owned more than 50 percent by another person."[3] This BEA measure of value added by the UBO does the best job of capturing the aspects of FDI activities that policymakers are most concerned with. However, it is not easily comparable to data collected by other countries. Thus this chapter presents data on FDI in the United States using both the balance of payments measure and the value added by UBO measure.

Figure 1.2 shows the top 20 largest sources of FDI flows in the United States in 2010, according to official US data computed using the balance of payments definition of direct investment. This approach allows for direct comparison of the numbers in figure 1.2 and the information in figure 1.1. By this measure, most direct investment in the United States comes from other highly developed nations. The top three are all European countries, with Japan ranking fourth. China is only the 18th largest source of FDI in the United States.

Figure 1.3 shows the value added of affiliates of foreign firms in the United States, classified by the country of ultimate ownership for 2009, the most recent year for which these data are available. These data are preferable to the balance of payments measures in figure 1.2 for reasons discussed above. However, they are less comparable to the numbers in figure 1.1 because they were computed using a methodology that most other countries have not adopted. Even with the methodological differences, the top seven or eight countries account for the vast majority of direct investment in the United States and are similar across the two tables—excepting Luxembourg, which is much more likely to be an immediate source than an ultimate owner for FDI. By this measure, China ranks 29th among direct investors in the United States.

Comparing Foreign Investors with US Firms in the United States: What the Data Say

Many apprehensions about the effects of foreign multinationals as they enter the United States—often by acquiring US companies—are based on empirical questions about the characteristics of foreign investors and their performance when they invest here. This is especially true for questions about employment, wages, trade, and the types of activities that foreign firms choose to locate in the United States in comparison to US companies. Previous studies, such as those of Edward Graham and Paul Krugman (1995) and Edward Graham and David Marchick (2006), have presented evidence that foreign-owned firms operating in the United States, including Japanese firms, actually performed better on a number of measures than US-owned firms. Figure 1.4 replicates their results using updated data.

The graphs in the figure show characteristics of three types of firms operating in the United States. The first bar of each graph provides information

---

3. See US Bureau of Economic Analysis, Foreign Direct Investment in the United States: Preliminary 2009 Statistics, 2011.

Figure 1.2 FDI flows to the United States, by source country, 2010

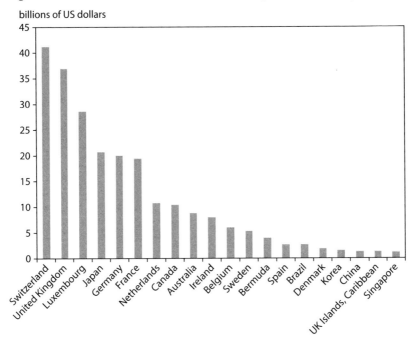

billions of US dollars

Source: US Bureau of Economic Analysis.

on all firms operating in the country, regardless of origin or ownership status. The second bar describes the operations of US-owned multinationals within the United States. The third bar shows the same information for majority-owned affiliates of foreign firms operating in the United States. As can be seen, the operations of foreign and US multinationals differ from those of domestic US firms in important ways. Multinational corporations (MNCs) have been shown to be more productive, pay higher wages, and have greater sales than purely domestic firms (Bernard and Jensen 1999). Figure 1.4 shows that foreign-owned firms are an important source of employment for US workers: Majority-owned US affiliates of foreign multinationals employed about 5.3 million Americans in 2009, the most recent data available.

Because the BEA collects its data using surveys of firms, the employment numbers for both US and foreign-owned multinationals may miss some hiring by small firms. The BEA gathers information from the entire universe of foreign firms operating in the United States only once every five years; it conducted its last comprehensive survey in 2007. In all other years, the BEA requires only firms above a certain size to respond to the survey and estimates the figures for smaller firms using a sampling technique. In 2009 all affiliates

Figure 1.3   Value added by US affiliates of foreign firms, by country of ultimate ownership, 2009

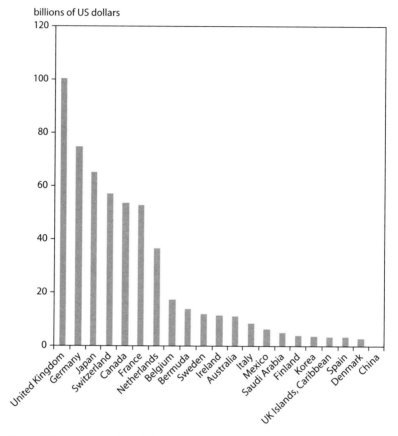

billions of US dollars

of foreign firms in the United States that had total assets, sales, or net income (or loss) of greater than $120 million were required to respond. A sample of firms below the $120 million cutoff was also surveyed, and responses from this sample were used to estimate total values for all firms. Because of the survey and sampling methodology, measurement error in the reported statistics is likely to be very small.

Based on the data, any lingering fear that foreign investors might only locate inferior, low-wage jobs in the United States is demonstrably inaccurate. Foreign investors in the United States pay higher wages on average than US employers—even US multinationals, which are among the highest paying of all US firms. The average worker at a US firm earned $64,552 in wages and benefits in 2009. Compensation was slightly higher for the US-based employees of

Figure 1.4   Operations of firms located in the United States, 2009

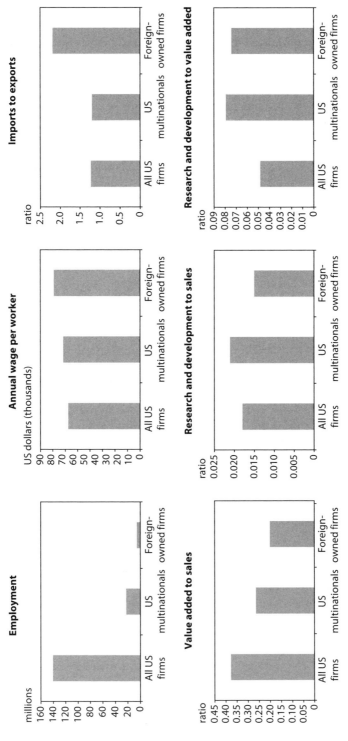

Employment

Annual wage per worker

Imports to exports

Value added to sales

Research and development to sales

Research and development to value added

Sources: US Bureau of Economic Analysis and US Census Bureau.

US-owned multinationals, who earned an average of $69,208 that year. The US-based employees of foreign-owned multinationals outearned both of these groups with an average income of $77,597. Studies of multinational activities pay a great deal of attention to the superior performance of US-owned multinationals relative to purely domestic firms. But they rarely look at wages in foreign-owned firms operating in the United States, which are much higher than even the most productive of US-owned firms.

It is possible that the higher average wages in foreign-owned firms in the United States could be due to selection bias if they reflect a difference in the types of industries that foreign and domestic firms specialize in. For example, if Japanese or European firms, say, are concentrated in the electronics sector and electronics firms pay higher wages than, say, home appliances regardless of ownership, then the data would not necessarily be showing Japanese or European firms locating the highest-wage jobs of that firm or industry in the United States, but instead the comparative numbers might simply reflect an industry composition effect. Though even if industry composition is the reason for higher wages, it is unclear why this should be troublesome from a US perspective. If foreign firms are creating high-paying jobs in the United States, why should it matter if this is because those firms are operating in high-wage industries or because they are locating the highest-paying jobs of an average industry in the United States?

Nonetheless, it is instructive to break the wage results down by subsector. Figure 1.5 plots the average wage paid to employees of foreign-owned firms in the United States operating in each subsector against the average wage paid to workers in all US firms in the same subsectors. Almost all the observations are above the 45-degree line in the graph, meaning that in these subsectors, foreign-owned firms on average paid higher wages than US firms. Table 1.1 presents additional data on the subsectors. In major manufacturing and other subsectors in which foreign-controlled firms have a significant presence, foreign firms paid higher annual wages and salaries than the average US firms in those subsectors did. In 2006, of the more than 5.3 million workers foreign-controlled firms employed in the United States, 2 million of them were in manufacturing.[4] In 10 of the 12 major manufacturing subsectors, foreign firms pay more than the overall US average wages and benefits in those subsectors. For example, the average worker at a machinery manufacturer in the United States earned $68,374 per year, while the average worker at a foreign-owned machinery manufacturer in the United States earned $74,459. For manufacturing sectors as a whole, the average annual income, including wages and benefits, of a US worker at a foreign-owned firm was more than $9,000 higher than the average worker across all firms. The only individual subsectors within manufacturing that this was not true of were computers and automotive assembly. The average computers or electronics worker in the United States

---

4. Data by subsector are not available for 2009, thus the most recent year with this level of detail, 2006, is used instead.

Figure 1.5 Average annual compensation per worker, by subsector, 2006

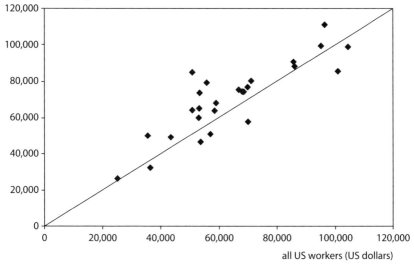

employees of foreign-owned firms in the United States (US dollars)

all US workers (US dollars)

Sources: Data on majority-owned affiliates of foreign investors are from the US Bureau of Economic Analysis; data on subsectors are from the US Census Bureau.

earns $100,701 per year, while the average worker at a foreign-owned computer or electronics company earned $85,697. Foreign-owned firms also paid higher than average wages in 9 of the 13 major nonmanufacturing categories. The finance and insurance industry had one of the biggest income gaps: Employees of foreign-owned firms in the United States earned $180,446, almost double the national average of $97,991. In paying higher than average wages in the aggregate and usually higher wages than US companies in the same industry pay, foreign investors in the United States create good jobs.

In R&D, figure 1.4 shows that foreign investors spend almost as much as average US firms do, when weighted by total sales. However, total sales may not be the best measure to look at R&D spending as a share of total activity. Total sales numbers do not reflect only production that takes place in the United States, but also include the value of intermediate inputs and production activities that have taken place in other countries. A better measure is value added, which includes only a firm's US activities and allows comparisons with the share of total US activities devoted to R&D. Thus figure 1.4 also presents R&D spending as a share of value added. US firms spend about 4.8 percent of value added on R&D, whereas the majority-owned affiliates of foreign investors spend more than 7 percent. This is somewhat surprising since MNCs might be expected to concentrate their R&D activities close to their worldwide headquarters: The US headquarters of US multinationals spend slightly more on

Table 1.1   Employment and wages by subsector, 2006

Subsector	Majority-owned affiliates of foreign investors in the United States		Entire subsector	
	Average compensation per employee (US dollars)	Number of workers (thousands)	Average compensation per employee (US dollars)	Number of workers (thousands)
All industries, total	68,257	5,334	58,854	119,917
Manufacturing, total	75,665	2,064	66,595	13,632
Food	64,387	128	50,749	1,459
Beverages and tobacco	85,130	39	50,749	155
Textiles and apparel	49,505	18	43,341	598
Paper	77,037	38	69,725	441
Printing	60,180	28	52,936	641
Chemicals	111,312	297	96,184	805
Plastics and rubber	65,349	116	53,103	901
Nonmetallic mineral	64,097	173	58,358	482
Machinery	74,459	213	68,374	1,127
Computers and electronics	85,697	169	100,701	1,057
Electrical equipment	74,575	84	67,853	420
Motor vehicles and parts	58,030	316	69,864	1,008
Wholesale trade	80,426	615	70,943	6,031
Retail trade	32,739	564	36,269	15,768
Information services	88,214	226	85,898	3,396
Finance and insurance	180,446	215	97,991	6,647
Real estate and leasing	73,909	44	53,237	2,217
Professional, scientific, and technical	90,940	202	85,504	8,054
Computer systems design	99,177	67	104,126	1,215
Agriculture, forestry, and fishing	50,339	6	35,417	166
Mining	99,727	77	94,946	554
Construction	79,423	75	55,656	7,339
Transportation and warehousing	51,210	233	56,911	4,306
Health care	46,869	81	53,571	16,451
Accommodation and food service	26,811	358	25,118	11,381

Sources: Data on majority-owned affiliates of foreign investors in the United States are from the US Bureau of Economic Analysis; data on entire subsectors are from the US Census Bureau.

R&D than do affiliates of foreign MNCs operating in the United States. That foreign firms spend so much on R&D in the United States suggests that they are not overwhelmingly motivated to keep high value-added activities near their home headquarters. International companies locate production activities where they will be performed the most effectively, and the abundance of highly educated workers and friendly environment for research and innovation in the United States make it a desirable place to locate those activities, whatever the nationality of the parent.

Foreign firms in the United States do differ significantly from US-owned firms in their net imports. On average, firms located in the United States import more than they export, regardless of ownership, but affiliates of foreign firms do this to a greater extent. Is this something the United States should worry about? The appropriate answer is no. Imports are not necessarily undesirable; a higher propensity to import is likely to mean that foreign affiliates simply have better access to more efficient external supply chains than US-based firms do—a phenomenon one also sees when US multinationals in Europe import more from the United States than they export from their host countries. Importing allows foreign firms engaging in FDI to be more competitive in the United States, and at least partly undergirds their ability to pay higher than average wages to US workers and provide high-quality products to US consumers. Moreover, as pointed out in the next chapter, multinational investors are an important source of imported intermediates, which account for about one-third of all productivity gains in the US workforce, leading firms and workers to be more competitive at home and in export markets.

In addition, much of the relatively large volume of foreign firms' imports can be explained by their role in facilitating wholesale trade. The trade gap for affiliates of foreign firms can be largely accounted for by wholesale trade affiliates, many of which were established to facilitate the import of goods manufactured abroad by their foreign parents. Many of the manufacturing affiliates in the data also have secondary activities in wholesale trade, and many of them import parts and components that their foreign parents produce.[5] This pattern produces the relatively lower value added to sales ratio of foreign firms in the United States compared with the set of all US-based firms.

As for trade balance, macroeconomic factors, and not the behavior of individual firms, determine a country's current account balance and its unemployment rate. By definition, the US current account deficit is the difference between domestic investment and domestic savings, so a deficit reflects a low level of US saving. Another way to express the balance of payments accounting equation is to note that the US current account deficit represents the difference between what the United States spends and what it earns, with the balance being financed with credit from foreigners. As long as the US public and private sectors spend more than the United States earns, there will always be a need for foreign financing, no matter what individual US firms do with regard to exports or imports. Individual firm behavior cannot affect the current account balance unless it somehow affects the demand for savings or investment (as is quite possible).

A potentially more valid source of concern over high net imports is the effect that they may have on exchange rates, as the exchange rate may adjust to offset net imports. To determine if foreign firms operating in the United States significantly affect exchange rates through the net imports channel,

---

5. See US Bureau of Economic Analysis, Foreign Direct Investment in the United States: Preliminary 2009 Statistics, 2011.

it is necessary to investigate whether having these firms in the United States increases or decreases US imports. About 7 percent of the total sales by foreign firms operating in the United States are exports, meaning that the vast majority of their sales are to local US consumers. Consider the case of Toyota. In 2006 the company began manufacturing its Camry and Tundra models at a plant in Lafayette, Indiana. These were not new products introduced in the Lafayette plant to compete with domestic brands; they were car and truck models that Americans had already been buying. The only difference was that now they were assembled in Indiana rather than in Japan or at a Toyota factory in another country. In this hypothetical case, FDI actually reduces imports. Were it not for the presence of these firms, US consumers might well (hypothetically) import many of these products from their countries of origin rather than buying them locally. The alternative to buying from a foreign firm located in the United States is probably not purchasing a purely domestic good with every component made by a US-owned firm. Rather, the choice may be between purchasing a good from a foreign firm in the United States versus importing it from abroad. Thus the net impact of the presence of foreign firms on US imports could be net positive or net negative and cannot be precisely predicted either way.

Those concerned about the effects of foreign investment in the United States have sometimes suggested that foreign firms might be bad for US workers because they favor states with weak worker protections when deciding where to invest. This could pressure state governments to weaken labor protection laws in order to attract foreign investment. However, there is little evidence that foreign firms exhibit such a bias. Norman Glickman and Douglas Woodward (1991) show that labor climate—their measurement of a combination of low unionization rates, right to work laws, and low strike activity—strongly influenced the location of foreign firm employment in the 1970s but that this "antiunion bias" was reversed in the 1980s, with foreign firm employment positively associated with the rate of unionization in a state. Today US affiliates of foreign multinationals have higher unionization rates than the rest of the US private sector. In 2007, 8.9 percent of US employees of foreign-owned firms were covered by collective bargaining agreements versus 8.2 percent of all private sector workers in the United States (Anderson and Zeile 2009).

As noted at the beginning of this chapter, preoccupations about foreign investment in the United States in the 1980s and 1990s focused on the comparative behavior of Japanese firms as they set up operations in the US market. Reviewing how Japanese MNC behavior in the US market has evolved offers conclusions that inform the current debate on FDI in the United States, which now focuses on developing countries, such as China. Looking at a subset of Japanese investors, Graham and Krugman (1995) and Graham and Marchick (2006) found that Japanese investors in the United States paid higher wages and benefits, invested more in R&D, and had greater value added than average US firms. Sector by sector, however, the picture the authors painted was more

**Figure 1.6   Research and development spending by affiliates of
              Japanese firms in the United States, 1977–2009**

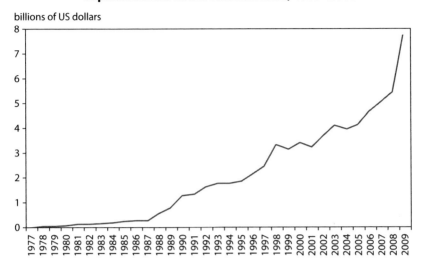

Source: US Bureau of Economic Analysis.

nuanced. They noted that wages and benefits in the transportation industry
were slightly lower than at comparable US firms, which might seem at first
like a matter of concern. But over time this may have made the US affiliates
of the Japanese corporations more competitive in the face of international
trade competition than the struggling traditional Big Three (Ford, General
Motors, and Chrysler)—good news for the US workers employed at those
Japanese firms in the United States. Japanese imports tended to be higher
than those of domestic firms, perhaps because of *keiretsu* relationships, but US
domestic content among Japanese car assemblers grew appreciably (Graham
and Krugman 1995). The R&D expenditures of Japanese investors started out
at lower levels than comparable US firms but grew larger the longer Japanese
firms remained in the US market. Overall, the studies conclude that fears
about the potential negative consequences of Japanese FDI in the United States
were unfounded. Figure 1.6 shows the growth of R&D spending by Japanese
firms in the United States.

FDI in the United States over Time

The previous section presented a snapshot of foreign firms operating in the
United States compared with both US-owned multinationals and purely
domestic US firms. This section looks at how the activities of foreign firms in
the United States have evolved over time. Does the evidence show any secular
decline in foreign investors' contributions to the US job base, worker earnings,
or R&D efforts? The data from foreign investors offer some unexpected results,
even during the recent recession. Figure 1.7 shows trends in the activities of

Figure 1.7 Operations of majority-owned affiliates of foreign firms in the United States, 1997–2009

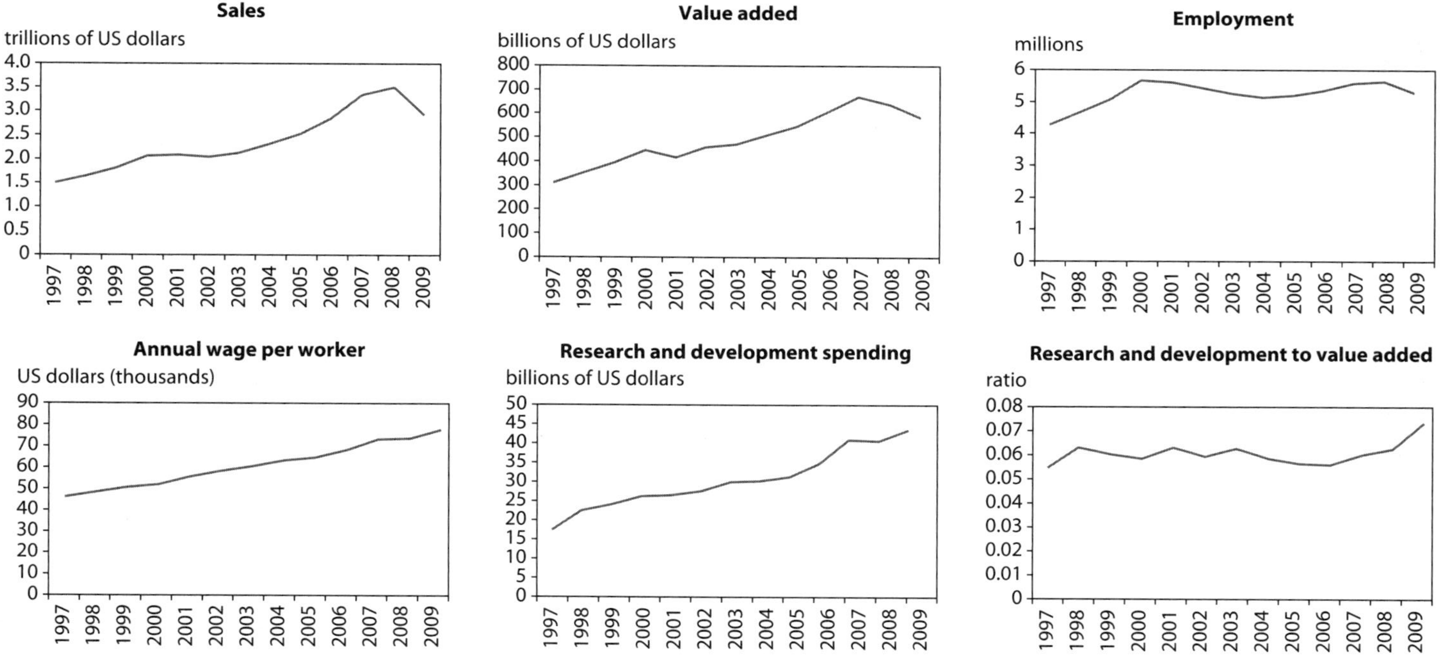
Sales
trillions of US dollars
4.0
3.5
3.0
2.5
2.0
1.5
1.0
0.5
0
Value added
billions of US dollars
800
700
600
500
400
300
200
100
0
Employment
millions
6
5
4
3
2
1
0
Annual wage per worker
US dollars (thousands)
90
80
70
60
50
40
30
20
10
0
Research and development spending
billions of US dollars
50
45
40
35
30
25
20
15
10
5
0
Research and development to value added
ratio
0.08
0.07
0.06
0.05
0.04
0.03
0.02
0.01
0
1997
1998
1999
2000
2001
2002
2003
2004
2005
2006
2007
2008
2009

Source: US Bureau of Economic Analysis.

majority-owned affiliates of foreign firms in the United States from 1997 to 2009. Over this time period, sales, value added, employment, wages, and R&D spending all increased. Not surprisingly, the firms' sales and employment dipped slightly along with overall US economic activity during the 2009 recession. From 2008 to 2009 US GDP fell by 2.5 percent and total private sector employment contracted by 5.3 percent. During that same time, sales by foreign firms in the United States fell by 17 percent and US employment at the firms fell by 6.3 percent. However, sales and employment by foreign-owned firms in the United States had grown at a much faster pace than the overall economy in the years before the recession, resulting in long-term positive trends. More surprising is the strong growth in wages paid by foreign firms in the United States, even during the recession: The average annual wage paid to US employees of foreign-owned firms grew by almost 6 percent from 2008 to 2009. During this same period, average wages for the US private sector grew by only 2.7 percent.

With sales contracting, what drove wage growth? As figure 1.7 shows, foreign firms' R&D spending in the United States was very strong and expanded during the recession. From 2008 to 2009, R&D by foreign firms in the United States increased in both absolute volume and as a share of value added. Together these figures show a trend of strong growth in the operations of foreign-owned firms in the United States. Predictably, certain activities such as sales and employment by these firms suffered during the 2009 recession. However, R&D and wages remained strong. Data for the period after the recession are not yet available, but there is no reason to expect that the operations of foreign firms in the United States will not bounce back, especially given these firms' strong investment in R&D during the recession.

The preceding comparisons help assuage concerns about negative consequences when foreign investors take over US firms or otherwise invest in the United States. But they also suggest that FDI can be a source of important benefits to the host economy. Why might this be so, and what kinds of benefits might be reasonable to expect? To answer this, it is important to review the relatively new explanations for what motivates FDI, particularly in manufacturing and services.

2

Rationale and Motivation for FDI: Why Do Foreign Companies Invest in the United States?

In recent years economists have made many important strides toward better understanding and modeling the role of firms in international trade. Today careful measurement of potential benefits from foreign direct investment (FDI) requires appreciating the dynamic interactions among trade, investment, and technology as multinational firms cross borders. This chapter opens with an overview of these new insights. The starting point is still the foundation laid out by Adam Smith and David Ricardo: Traditional conceptions of international comparative advantage in which nations trade on the basis of relative endowments of land, labor, and capital—including relative endowments of higher-skilled versus lower-skilled labor—remain indispensable. All trading partners are better off if they do more of what they do best and their firms enjoy economies of scale and specialization. The win-win outcome from exchanging wine for wool, and vice versa, still holds.

But new micro-level theories and evidence about trade show that gains also come from dynamic sorting among firms within industries, not only from one-time shifts in production activity along lines of factor endowment–based comparative advantage.[1] Apple still has to consider how to allocate assembly operations among China, Vietnam, and the Philippines as wages rise in China, a problem well understood within the Smith-Ricardo framework (not to mention Heckscher-Ohlin). But the tremendous dynamism that drives Apple in new directions comes from managers and engineers waking up each morning and wondering what Ericsson, Samsung, Nokia, and Huawei, among

---

1. For theoretical modeling, see Melitz (2003). For empirical evidence, see Bernard and Jensen (1999), Pavcnik (2002), Bernard, Jensen, and Schott (2005), Bernard et al. (2003), or Verhoogen (2007).

others, are going to introduce into the market, and at what cost. The same pressures simultaneously drive component makers around the world, from producers of microprocessors and semiconductors to manufacturers of hard drives and batteries. This competitive thrust within industries is a continuous real-time impetus for innovation, not a very slowly evolving change in comparative advantage.

The new appreciation of the dynamic forces of competition, technological and managerial innovation through imitation, and new research and development (R&D) discoveries—along with shifts among worker tasks and skill levels—highlights the importance of individual firm behavior and policies that allow individual firms to excel. Looking only at aggregate data and not at micro-level evidence masks the tremendous amount of churning that occurs within sectors; access to more detailed data and the ever-growing sophistication of modeling techniques confirms the role of individual firms in determining the direction and volume of, as well as the potential gains from, international trade. When allowed to compete freely, the firms that are best able to innovate and become more efficient expand their market share while less productive firms contract, resulting in ongoing net increases in overall productivity from exposure to international trade. Firm-level performance builds up and amplifies the natural advantages that already exist, imparting welfare gains on a continuous basis. Policies to create an environment in which firms can perform at their peak in rivalry with each other thus are vital to realizing the full benefits of trade for workers, input producers of goods and services, consumers, communities, and overall standards of living.

The importance of firm-level performance to economywide gains is even more important when flows of goods, services, technology, management, and quality control take place within single multinational corporate networks. The speed and intimacy of intra-affiliate interaction dwarfs what occurs in arm's-length trade transactions. Yet despite the increased understanding of the role of firms in imports and exports, much less progress has been made in modeling the complex FDI decisions of multinational firms. Over the past three decades, the role of FDI has grown rapidly with the expansion of the world economy. As world nominal GDP has increased four times and world bilateral trade flows have grown more than sixfold, the FDI stock has swelled by roughly 20 times from an already reasonably large base in 1980. Today the global sales of foreign affiliates of multinational corporations (MNCs) are roughly twice the amount of total world exports, making foreign investors considerably more important than trade in delivering goods and services around the globe. Within the realm of trade, MNCs are the largest players in arm's-length transactions, while one-third of transfers of goods and services across borders take place within their intrafirm networks. MNCs account for about half the world's total R&D expenditure and more than two-thirds of the world's business R&D. The bulk of technology flows between countries takes place within the confines of multinational investor production systems. From today's vantage point, it thus may be difficult to appreciate how recent any rigorous understanding of the rationale and motivation for FDI has been, and how perplexing the phenomenon of FDI has seemed.

Why Do Firms Engage in FDI?

The key to understanding the motivation for manufacturing and services FDI emerged in the 1960s and 1970s from a small group of insightful researchers, including Stephen Hymer, Charles Kindleberger, Raymond Vernon, and John H. Dunning. These breakthrough intellectual figures, their collaborators, and their students began to understand FDI flows as the awkwardly phrased but analytically brilliant internalization of intangible assets: Functioning as an alternative to exporting or licensing, FDI is a strategy to maintain or extend a firm's ability to maximize profits by controlling and integrating operations across borders. Firms can gain advantages through ownership, location, and internalization. Ownership advantages are those that the firm itself possesses and would not be able to enjoy simply by trading at arm's length with another firm. These include attributes such as the company's reputation, brand recognition, production techniques, entrepreneurial and management skills, and internal returns to scale. Location advantages are all the benefits associated with producing in a certain country and include traditional sources of comparative advantage, such as low-skilled labor abundance (or high-skilled labor abundance and R&D potential), natural resources, government incentives such as tax breaks or tariffs, and proximity to consumers. Internalization advantages are any benefits that come from keeping production within the firm rather than using licensing or joint ventures. Much of this line of reasoning is based on the Nobel Prize–winning work of Oliver Williamson, who showed that firms can overcome many of the problems associated with imperfect contracting and other challenges of legal enforcement associated with doing business across borders by internalizing their suppliers.

More recently, a branch of international economics has emerged to formalize and add to the ideas of Hymer, Kindleberger, Vernon, Dunning, and Williamson with regard to manufacturing and services FDI. While most multinational manufacturing and services corporations engage in complex production strategies, the formal theoretical and empirical literature has often found it useful to break the main components down into separate categories depending on the primary motive for FDI. This allows for rigorous study of each channel, independent of complicating circumstances. The most common of these channels are known as vertical, horizontal, and export platform FDI. In practice, most firms engage in some combination of them, but considering them separately helps in understanding firms' many different motives for investment.

Vertical FDI focuses on how firms choose to source inputs and separate production activities across borders. In this case, the production process is fragmented into its various components, which can each take place in a different country. Generally, more complex and strategic aspects of production, such as management and product design, take place at the firm's headquarters in this model while more routine tasks, such as production or assembly of inputs, occur at foreign affiliates (Oldenski 2012). Vertical FDI occurs most often when a firm's headquarters country and affiliate country differ in their skill endowments and wages. A US automaker moving production and assembly of parts to Mexico to take advantage of abundant low-wage labor is a typical example, as FDI facilitates trade within the firm.

Elhanan Helpman (1984) was one of the first economists to develop a model for vertical FDI. In his framework, firms can source inputs in any location to minimize costs. As a result, each stage of multinational production takes place where there is a comparative advantage in that production activity. Robert Feenstra and Gordon Hanson (1997) developed a similar model and found empirical support for it using data on US firms operating in Mexico. James Markusen (1997) showed that the existence of the motive for vertical FDI suggests that liberalizing investment policies can increase trade volumes along with multinational investment, as firms trade large volumes of inputs among their various geographic locations.

Export platform FDI is similar to vertical FDI in that it fragments production and facilitates trade. Under this type of multinational organization, a firm headquartered in one country locates production in a second country to serve consumers in a third country, usually to take advantage of low tax rates or abundant inputs. For example, Ireland often has been chosen in the past as a location for export platform FDI due to its low corporate tax rates and proximity to EU countries. Karolina Ekholm, Rikard Forslid, and James Markusen (2007) show that free trade areas promote this type of FDI, as when US firms locate production in Mexico for export to third countries. Monika Mrázová and Peter Neary (2011) view export platform FDI as an intermediate option that combines aspects of both trade and investment. It is widely known that FDI involves greater initial startup costs than exporting, as firms making direct investments must spend large amounts of capital building or acquiring a foreign affiliate. Because FDI is so costly, only the most efficient firms find it worthwhile to establish a branch plant in each country. The least efficient firms do not become multinationals, keeping operations in only one country and exporting from there. Firms of intermediate efficiency may establish one foreign affiliate to use as an export platform. Thus it is reasonable to expect firms using export platform FDI to be more productive than purely domestic firms, but not quite as productive as multinationals with a larger number of affiliates.

Under the model of horizontal FDI, firms open foreign affiliates not to produce inputs but to get closer to customers. Horizontal FDI is often framed as an alternative to trade: When a firm headquartered in one country wants to sell its products to consumers in another country, it can do so by producing at home and exporting or by opening up an affiliate branch in the destination market and producing there. Paul Krugman (1983), Ignatius Horstmann and James Markusen (1992), and Lael Brainard (1993, 1997) show that horizontal FDI is more cost effective than trade when the cost of exporting is high due to tariffs or transport costs. It is also more likely to occur in large markets, where the potential local sales are significant enough to cover the high cost of opening a foreign affiliate. The productivity level of the firm matters, too. Elhanan Helpman, Marc Melitz, and Stephen Yeaple (2004) show that only the most productive firms can cover the costs associated with becoming a multinational. Less productive firms rely on exports or purely domestic sales.

As mentioned above, most firms engage in more than one of the three types of FDI. Markusen (1997) and David Carr, James Markusen, and Keith Maskus (2001) develop what they refer to as the knowledge capital model of multinational enterprises, which integrates these types of FDI into one model. Under their framework, the activities multinationals engage in can be divided into two categories: knowledge-based and production activities. Knowledge-based activities include core functions, such as R&D and management, which are generally high-skill-intensive and take place at the firm's headquarters. Production activities are low-skill-intensive and can be geographically separated from knowledge-based activities. Firms decide how many production affiliates to have and in which countries they should be located. Carr, Markusen, and Maskus (2001) find that vertical structures (e.g., separation of knowledge and production work) are more likely to occur when the countries differ in their endowments of skilled and unskilled labor. Horizontal structures (e.g., duplication of production activities) are more likely when countries are similar in terms of GDP and levels of consumer demand.

The models of horizontal, vertical, and export platform FDI, as well as the incorporation of all three types under the knowledge capital model, are useful to understand certain forms of direct investment. But they do not address important patterns observed in the behavior of actual firms, such as the fragmentation of R&D activities around the world. Access to consumers and low cost inputs are not the only motive for FDI; knowledge seeking also plays an important role. Looking at the variation in activities of foreign-owned firms across US states, Wilbur Chung and Juan Alcacer (2002) find that firms in research-intensive industries, such as pharmaceuticals, are more likely to locate in states with high R&D intensity. This is true of firms from both developed and developing countries. Such behavior cannot be explained by traditional models, which rely on a somewhat outdated conception of how multinationals operate. They generally conceive of a firm with one headquarters located in its country of origin, where all high-value activities, such as R&D and management, take place, and a number of pure production facilities in other countries that simply implement the ideas generated at headquarters. This is not consistent with the data showing foreign investors in the United States engaged in large-scale, ever-deepening R&D activities around the country. International firms that create highly integrated corporate networks across borders and allow for seamless production coordination and near-simultaneous knowledge upgrades also defy the standard models. Future work by us will discuss this gap between theory and practice in greater detail and outline a new framework for conceptualizing FDI flows in an increasingly real-time integrated production strategy.

Until now, there also has been very little systematic analysis of why nonresource international companies headquartered in developing countries would engage in uphill FDI by investing in high-income countries like the United States. This study suggests motivations far removed from traditional concepts such as relative wage rates or access to capital. Nonresource MNCs from emerging markets, such as China, seek out developed-world sites as a better location for management and research than their home economies and avail themselves of the benefits of proximity to rich consumers. Finally, in addition to motives for FDI based purely on increasing productivity and efficiency within the firm, multinationals also contend with a number of more strategic and policy-based incentives: MNCs can use direct investment to jump over tariff barriers, a fact well known by governments that set tariffs in part with an eye toward increasing investment.

However, even with the shortcomings of existing frameworks in addressing the full spectrum of motives for FDI, certain aspects of these frameworks for understanding the dynamics of multinational manufacturing and service investment can help to explain some of the empirical outcomes—and beneficial effects—observed in the preceding chapter, though some modifications are needed. Theories of multinational firms suggest that foreign companies are drawn to the United States by the presence of highly skilled knowledge workers, and that any firm that is able to invest internationally in the first place must have already achieved a high level of productivity. The data support these claims, suggesting that foreign firms that build plants and set up offices in the United States are not simply average, or even better than average, contributors to the US economy, but extraordinarily valuable contributors. In 2006, majority-owned US affiliates of foreign multinationals owned $5.5 trillion in assets, produced $515 billion of goods and services within the United States, and accounted for 6.1 percent of total US private value added, up from 3.8 percent in 1988, the first year for which data are available (Anderson 2008). US affiliates of foreign multinationals employed 5.3 million workers, or 4.6 percent of the US workforce, up from 3.5 percent in 1988. From an output base of 6 percent of the US total, they account for a disproportionately large share of US exports (19 percent), physical capital expenditures (10 percent), and R&D expenditures (14 percent; see Bernard, Jensen, and Schott 2005).

In addition, as theory predicts and evidence confirms, foreign investors in the United States spend more on R&D in the United States than other similar firms. They are only slightly behind the rate of R&D expenditures of US parents of US multinationals, the most R&D intensive of all firms in the United States (Graham and Marchick 2006). In some subsectors—such as computer manufacturing and communications equipment, which includes telecommunications equipment—the affiliates of foreign firms spend a greater portion of value added on R&D than US parents of multinationals in the same subsector do. In light of this, a logical next question is to ask what effects these and other activities may have on the US economy.

Effect of FDI on the Host Country

FDI can be thought of as one type of international trade, bringing about many of the same benefits as any other form of trade. The most obvious of these benefits comes from specialization based on comparative advantage. When each country or region focuses on the production of goods and services for which it is relatively most efficient, the overall efficiency of global production increases. In each country, resources are allocated to the activities for which they are most productive. Most of the industries in which multinationals operate exhibit increasing returns, that is, production is more efficient at a larger scale. By expanding across borders, firms can take advantage of these efficiencies, resulting in lower unit costs, the benefits of which can be shared with workers and passed along to consumers as lower prices. In the United States, foreign-owned plants are more capital intensive, are more productive in both labor and total factor productivity (output generated for a given quantity of land, labor, and other inputs), use a higher proportion of nonproduction workers, and pay higher wages than the average US-owned plant. Controlling for industry, size, age, and state (location), foreign-owned plants in the United States still show superior operating characteristics compared with domestically owned plants. Foreign-owned plants in the United States pay wages 2.5 to 7 percent higher than comparable domestic plants do (Doms and Jensen 1998). David Figlio and Bruce Blonigen (2000) find that foreign investor firms raise local real wages more than domestic firms do. The data in figures 1.4 and 1.5 in the previous chapter echo these results: FDI raises US living standards by improving access to good jobs.

But FDI represents transfers of technology, management, quality control, and marketing know-how across borders that is much more intimate and potent than arm's-length trade, a phenomenon that the economics and policy communities are just beginning to recognize (Moran 2011). Multinational firms that set up intrafirm supplier links among affiliates in different countries behave differently in significant ways from those that do not. In an analysis of the relations between US parents and their affiliates in 49 developing countries from 1983 to 1996, Susan Feinberg and Michael Keane (2005) find that knowledge flows, production coordination, reporting links, and other communication channels are more extensive and active between the affiliates and the parent, and among the affiliates themselves, for firms that are organized to engage in intrafirm trade than for firms with little or no intrafirm trade. In relations between US multinational parents and their Canadian manufacturing affiliates, Feinberg and Keane find that factors associated with the intimacy of their interaction—concurrent engineering, just-in-time inventory control, computer-based logistics management, statistical quality control, and total quality management—are, surprisingly, much more important in explaining growth in trade than either tariff reductions or declines in transportation costs. An emerging body of literature on the role of culture and communication within multinationals suggests that knowledge and complex production processes can be transferred across borders much more efficiently within a firm than through arm's-length trade. Drawing on earlier theoretical work by Herbert Simon (1951), Oliver Williamson (1985), and Steven Tadelis (2002), Arnaud Costinot, Lindsay Oldenski, and James Rauch (2011) have shown empirically that by keeping international supply chains within the firm, multinationals can overcome many of the barriers associated with fragmenting complex processes across borders.

As multinational investors build corporate networks across borders, a degree of intimacy develops between parent and affiliate that is far different from the trading of goods and services among independent parties. Industry case studies demonstrate this phenomenon. For each new generation of disk drives, Seagate or Read-Rite brings more than a dozen process engineers and managers from wholly owned plants in Asia to meet with product developers at US headquarters 50 days before launch, followed two weeks later by 24 production supervisors to get a pilot line up and running. Then the entire new product transfer team returns to Asia, together with 10 to 20 engineers and managers from US headquarters to set up the actual production lines. This entire crew remains in place to troubleshoot the lines until the sites in Asia reach full capacity with low rejection rates. This back-and-forth sequence from headquarters to overseas affiliates is repeated for each disk-drive upgrade (McKendrick, Donner, and Haggard 2000).

But confirmation of close parental supervision over global production networks does not emerge solely from industry case studies. Across fourteen sectors as diverse as chemicals, medical products, metal products, rubber, food, transportation equipment, and electronics, Vijaya Ramachandran (1993) finds that the number of parent company employees sent to overseas affiliates to coordinate production and the number of overseas employees sent to the parent country for training is significantly higher when the affiliate is part of a wholly owned supplier network than in the case of joint venture, licensee, or arm's-length trading relationships. This intimacy among multinational corporate affiliates is reflected in their close coordination of production and design, special attention to quality control, and the speed and continuousness of upgrading technology and production techniques. It can be seen in companies in the high-performance electronics sector, such as Seagate and Read-Rite; it is also apparent in the automotive industry, as Volkswagen or General Motors plants in Eastern Europe produce engines, cylinder heads, and gearboxes that are interchangeable with corresponding output from facilities in Spain, Austria, and Germany, with the capability that facilities in all four countries can be upgraded simultaneously in real time.

The benefits from transfers of technology, production know-how, and quality control across borders with multinational investor networks show up in four ways. First, multinational investors bring new or cheaper products and services to consumers and increase competition in the domestic market for those products and services. Second, multinational investors bring new or cheaper intermediates to local firms, increasing competition in the domestic market for those intermediates and making local firms more competitive. Third, multinational investors reveal technologies, production know-how, and quality control techniques that rivals can imitate in the domestic market, resulting in spillovers that improve those rivals' performance. Fourth, multinational investors set up vertical supply chains, which they support with design specifications, production recommendations, quality control advice, and sales-backed financing. Often these suppliers move beyond captive status to become certified as original equipment manufacturer sellers to the entire industry, a vertical spillover externality. Across these four channels of effects on the host economy, the movement of goods, services, management techniques, technology, and quality control is faster—according to all available indicators—than it is for other kinds of non-FDI-integrated transactions.

For new or cheaper products and services for consumers, and increased competition in the domestic market, Scott Bradford, Paul Grieco, and Gary Hufbauer (2005) estimate that the US economy has grown richer by $1 trillion per year from liberalization of trade and investment since the end of World War II. This translates to about $9,000 per year for each American household, leaving the average US citizen about 10 percent more prosperous as a result of the globalization of trade and investment. All income groups, and small and medium-sized enterprises as well as larger firms, share in these benefits. In accounting for this, traditional models of trade and investment liberalization emphasize differences across countries in factor endowments and differing degrees of competitive advantage across industries because of these endowments. New models of global market integration, using micro-level firm data, show that differences across firms within an industry are much larger and more important than differences among industries or countries in factor endowments (Bernard and Jensen 1999). Sifting and sorting among firms within an industry dwarfs among-sector differences in performance in generating welfare gains in the domestic economy. For the United States, where most inward foreign investment represents intraindustry competition, FDI thus is likely to be a particularly important channel in producing this $1 trillion gain from liberalization of trade and investment. The dynamic effect from increased competition in the domestic market is particularly potent because it forces domestic firms to upgrade their technologies, managerial practices, and marketing techniques continuously. In contrast to the one-time adjustments that accompany conventional relocation of economic activities among countries due to different factor abundance, the stimulation of international competition among firms within an industry drives innovation in all countries every day and over time. This pressure to innovate can lead firms to discover new technologies and more efficient production processes on their own—or, as discussed later, can allow firms to observe and imitate the behavior of their competitors and then improve on it.

Regarding the introduction of new or cheaper inputs into the domestic market, intermediate imports have been growing much faster than imports of final products since the 1960s. David Hummels, Jun Ishii, and Kei-Mu Yi (2001) show that about one-third of the total growth in world trade that occurred between 1970 and 1990 can be attributed to growth in imports of intermediate inputs. Alexander Yeats (2001) estimates that intermediates account for about 30 percent of all world trade in manufactures. Some of these imports of intermediates are from arm's-length suppliers, but the majority of them are traded within multinational firms. This growth in imported intermediates has been linked to overall US productivity growth. David Richardson and David Huether (2001) estimate that intermediate import deepening represents more than one-third of the total increase in output per worker in the United States from the 1960s to the present. As FDI represents the largest source of growth in intermediate imports, it is a main source for growing productivity and enhancing the competitiveness of firms and workers in the United States. Regarding spillovers from foreign investors to domestic firms, as mentioned above, foreign investors in the United States spend more on R&D in the United States than other similar firms and only slightly less than US parents of US multinationals.

FDI has further economic implications beyond immediate job creation and R&D spending. The presence of foreign firms may also indirectly affect domestic firms. When foreign firms enter a market, they bring with them new production technologies and management practices that can spill over to the local market. Empirically identifying these spillovers and sorting out the causal relationship between FDI and productivity changes in neighboring firms is extremely difficult because FDI patterns reflect decisions firms have made, which may be influenced by their own expectations about future productivity growth in a given industry or region. However, a number of different studies have tackled this topic using various methodologies and almost all find some evidence of positive spillovers.

FDI spillovers can take the form of horizontal technology transfers from foreign to domestic firms in the same industry. Workers leaving a foreign-owned firm may take the techniques that they have learned there to their next job in a domestic firm. A number of studies have documented examples from Singapore, Taiwan, Hong Kong, Brazil, and Mexico, in which alumni of US and European firms have appeared on the management rosters of local companies (Pack 1997, Katz 1987). Domestic firms also may learn by observing their competitors. In a survey conducted by Beata Javorcik and Mariana Spatareanu (2005), one-quarter of the managers of Czech firms and 15 percent of the managers of Latvian firms reported that they gained knowledge about new technologies by studying foreign firms as those firms entered their industry. Twelve percent of the Czech managers and 9 percent of the Latvian managers added that they learned new marketing techniques and discovered new sales outlets by scrutinizing the foreign firms' behavior.

Spillovers may also be vertical. If foreign-owned firms wish to source inputs locally, they may demand higher quality or share production technology with their suppliers, resulting in greater productivity of local firms in upstream industries. Javorcik and Spatareanu find that direct assistance between foreigners and local suppliers takes the form of training, help with setting up production lines, coaching in management strategy and financial planning, advance payment and other kinds of financing, assistance with quality control, and introduction to export markets. Most of the literature on spillovers discussed below focuses on this vertical channel.

Research on multinational spillovers focuses primarily on the presence of developed-country firms in less developed markets, which is when the gap between the technology level of the firm's headquarters location and the host country is the greatest, and thus the potential for gains may be the highest. Evidence of positive spillover effects from FDI has been found for Mexico (Blomström 1986, Kokko 1994), Mauritius (Rhee, Katterback, and White 1990), Malaysia (Rasiah 1995, Capanelli 1997), Indonesia (Blomström and Sjöholm 1999; Blalock and Gertler 2005, 2008), Lithuania (Javorcik 2004), Ghana (Görg and Strobl 2005), and Thailand (Kohpaiboon 2007, 2009). It is also logical to expect to find positive spillovers from FDI between two developed countries, which may be even better equipped to absorb such spillover effects if a relatively high level of technology is necessary to incorporate new knowledge. Recent papers have found evidence of FDI spillovers between developed countries using data on Japanese investment in the United States (Branstetter 2006) and investment by a number of countries in the United Kingdom (Haskel, Pereira, and Slaughter 2007).

Whether because of the R&D expenditures foreign investors make in the US economy or because of their imports of external R&D, it turns out that the inflows of foreign investment into the United States constitute an important channel for technology spillovers to domestic companies, especially in high-technology sectors. Wolfgang Keller and Stephen Yeaple (2009) calculate that between 8 and 19 percent of all manufacturing productivity growth among US firms between 1987 and 1996 was derived from the growing presence of non-US direct investors in the US economy. The positive effect is disproportionately large in US high-technology sectors, namely chemicals, computers and office equipment, electronic components, scientific instruments, and medical instruments.

Much of the growth in inward FDI has taken place in sectors other than those Keller and Yeaple examined. Matthew Adler and Gary Hufbauer (2008) take a broader view, using data from 1982 through 2006 and including the entire private US economy. They use the relationship between FDI and total factor productivity (TFP) spillovers found by Keller and Yeaple and extrapolate it over a larger number of industries and years to estimate that approximately 2.14 percent of the entire TFP increase across the United States, in the 25-year period from 1982 to 2006, can be explained by inward FDI, an annual TFP gain of about $46 billion. Combining the up-to-date timeframe of Adler and Hufbauer with the cutting-edge econometric techniques and firm-level data of Keller and Yeaple offers rigorous new evidence on the extent of FDI spillovers in the United States.

New Evidence on FDI Spillovers in the United States

This study updates previous work on multinational spillovers following the method in Keller and Yeaple (2009) but using more recent data. Keller and Yeaple considered FDI from 1987 to 1996. The current work includes information on the years 1987 through 2007.

This analysis uses two different sources of firm-level data. The first, Compustat, is publicly available and contains information on the financial operations of firms located in the United States. The second is confidential data from firm-level surveys of multinational activity in the United States, including the operations of US-owned MNCs and foreign-owned firms with operations in the United States, which is collected by the US Department of Commerce's Bureau of Economic Analysis (BEA). The BEA data are publicly available by country and industry, but the underlying firm-level data are confidential. The analysis below uses the confidential BEA data to construct measures of the share of US employment at affiliates of foreign firms at a highly disaggregated level.

The dependent variable in the analysis is firm-level TFP of US firms. If foreign firms are inducing greater efficiency in their domestic counterparts, by exposing them to new technology and business practices, demanding higher-quality inputs, or increasing competition, these effects should show up as changes in TFP, which essentially captures how efficiently firms use a given set of inputs. Firm-level data from the Compustat database are used to compute TFP. This dataset includes US firms that are purely domestic as well as those with multinational operations, as spillovers may affect both groups. TFP is computed using the method described by Steven Olley and Ariel Pakes (1996). This approach has several benefits, most notably that it allows for firm entry and exit and controls for the simultaneity of input choice and productivity. The TFP—how efficiently a firm i uses a given set of inputs at time t—is calculated as

$$tfp_{it} = y_{it} - \beta_k^{OP}k_{it} - \beta_l^{OP}l_{it} - \beta_m^{OP}m_{it}, \tag{2.1}$$

where y_{it} is the log of output and k_{it}, l_{it}, and m_{it} are the firm's log of capital, labor, and material inputs. β_k^{OP}, β_l^{OP}, and β_m^{OP} are the Olley-Pakes estimates of the capital, labor, and materials production function elasticities, or the contribution that each factor makes to total output. Conceptually, this measure of TFP is simply the difference between the actual output of a firm and the expected output given that firm's capital, labor, and material inputs. The expected effect of each input is calculated controlling for the endogeneity of productivity and input choice as well as the possibility of firm exit. Endogeneity is a problem if the outcome variable of interest, in this case TFP, also exerts a causal influence on the variable or variables that are supposedly being used to explain its level. In this case, the endogeneity problem would arise if a given firm's productivity level were not due solely to input choices but if its productivity level also influenced its choice of inputs. The Olley-Pakes method controls for and thus eliminates this problem.

The effect of FDI on the productivity of domestic firms is estimated using the following equation:

$$\Delta tfp_{ijt} = \beta_0 + \beta_1 \Delta fdi_{jt-1} + \beta_2 \Delta fdi_{jt-2} + \sum_n \gamma_n X_{ijt} + \delta_j + \delta_t + \varepsilon_{ijt} \qquad (2.2)$$

The independent variable of interest, Δfdi, is the change in the share of employment at US affiliates of foreign firms in total US employment by industry and year. Employment at foreign-owned firms is calculated using the BEA firm-level data, which are aggregated up to the three-digit Standard Industrial Classification (SIC) industry level. Total US employment by industry comes from the Bureau of Labor Statistics (BLS). This measure of FDI employment shares is lagged by one and two years (denoted $t-1$ and $t-2$). Lagging the change in FDI share is important for several reasons. First, it likely takes time for the spillover effects of FDI on domestic firms to materialize. Second, there may be endogeneity problems associated with using contemporaneous values. Endogeneity problems might arise in these calculations if FDI is attracted to industries in which firms exhibit high productivity growth, making it difficult to determine which direction the causality moved in: the presence of foreign firms leading to greater productivity among domestic firms or the existence of highly productive domestic firms attracting FDI. Including lagged variables helps sort this out by examining the effect of FDI in one year on the productivity of firms in that industry a year or two later. Ideally the analysis could include a purely external shock that would cause FDI volumes to increase for reasons completely unrelated to productivity. But because FDI is a choice individual firms make, no such external force exists. Without an exogenous shock, using FDI volumes in the past to explain the productivity growth of neighboring firms in the future is the next best solution. This approach is not perfect. It assumes that firms cannot predict the future productivity growth of certain industries or geographic areas and adjust FDI to anticipate it. However, given the available data, this is the best way to begin answering important questions about the relation between FDI and productivity spillovers.

The regressions also control for a number of other factors, X_{ijt}, that will likely affect TFP, including the firm's capacity utilization, R&D spending, markups above marginal cost, market share, and capital expenditures. Data on these firm-level characteristics are from Compustat. However, even with these controls, industries still differ in important ways—such as their use of technology or the ease with which their production can be fragmented across borders—that might affect both productivity growth and FDI. Omitting these characteristics could make it appear as though FDI were causing the productivity growth when, in reality, investment and productivity changes were both due to some omitted third variable. For this reason, industry-level fixed effects are included to control for unobservable industry characteristics. These fixed effects hold constant the identity of the industry, and thus all its defining characteristics, to ensure that these characteristics do not confound the analysis. Similarly, year fixed effects are included to control for macroeconomic factors and other characteristics that vary with time in the sample.

Table 2.1 shows the results of this exercise, which provide very strong evidence of positive spillovers from FDI into the United States. An increase in the share of US employment accounted for by foreign firms in a given industry is positively and significantly associated with growth in TFP, or how efficiently US firms use inputs in that industry. In other words, the presence of foreign firms makes domestic US firms more productive. This result holds for FDI lagged by both one and two years, but the magnitude of the effect is greater after two years, suggesting that the benefits of positive spillovers increase over time.

The effect of inward FDI on the productivity of US firms is extremely large. Using the coefficient values from table 2.1, a 1 percentage point increase in the share of total employees in an industry who work at foreign-owned firms in the United States increases the productivity of all firms in the industry by an average of 0.81 percent after one year and by 2.75 percent in the second year, or a total of more than 3.5 percent. This is greater than the effect Keller and Yeaple found for 1987 through 1996, suggesting that the relation between FDI and technology spillovers in the United States may have increased over time. To put the magnitude of the spillover effects in context, consider the total effect that inward FDI has had on US productivity growth over the past two decades. Overall, US TFP grew by about 25 percent from 1987 through 2007 (OECD 2011). Over that same period, employment at foreign-owned firms as a share of total US employment grew from about 3.8 to 4.6 percent, a 0.8 percentage point increase. Using the estimates from table 2.1, that implies that productivity spillovers from FDI alone are responsible for US TFP growth of about 3 percent (0.008*(0.81 + 2.75)) from 1987 to 2007. This 3 percent is more than one-tenth of the 25 percent US TFP growth over that period. In other words, productivity spillovers from inward FDI account for about 12 percent of the total productivity growth in the United States from 1987 to 2007.

The data do not provide enough information to disentangle the precise extent to which the spillovers are horizontal or vertical. Because the estimates look at productivity effects within industries, they capture the horizontal spillovers among competitor firms producing similar products within the same industry. They also capture some, but not all, vertical spillovers. The industry data are at a relatively aggregated level, dividing production activities into about 70 industries. Thus it is not possible to distinguish, for example, whether spillovers in the automotive industry are between competing firms both producing cars or between a car manufacturer and its auto parts supplier, both of which would be classified as belonging to the broadly defined automotive industry. Morever, if an auto manufacturer experiences positive productivity spillovers from a firm supplying inputs classified as a different industry—such as steel, rubber, or leather—this analysis does not capture those cross-industry spillover effects. Thus the results in this section likely underestimate the total magnitude of productivity spillovers resulting from inward FDI.

Table 2.1 Spillover effects of a change in the industry-level FDI employment share on total factor productivity of domestic firms

Variable	Model 1
ΔFDI, t–1	80.53***
	(30.28)
ΔFDI, t–2	274.59***
	(29.67)
Capacity utilization	−0.21***
	(0.07)
Research and development	0.22***
	(0.01)
Markup	6.09*
	(3.19)
Market share	371.73***
	(36.35)
Capx	−0.13***
	(0.003)
Industry fixed effects	yes
Year fixed effects	yes
R-squared	0.03
Number of observations	24,311
Dependent variable	Δtfp

Notes: *, **, and *** indicate significance at the 10, 5, and 1 percent levels, respectively. Standard errors clustered by industry year are in parentheses.

Source: See text for the methods used to compute these results.

The data clearly show, however, that the vast majority of the inward investment that conveys such advantages for the US economy originates almost entirely in other highly developed OECD countries. In 2009 the seven largest source countries for direct investment in the United States were the United Kingdom, Germany, Japan, Switzerland, Canada, France, and the Netherlands, which together accounted for more than 75 percent of all FDI activity in the United States (see figure 1.3 in chapter 1). For this reason, most studies of the effects of FDI on the US economy have focused on investment from other developed countries. Does the same hold true for inward FDI from developing countries, including China?

3

Chinese FDI in the United States

China's emergence as a major player in the international economy cannot help but inspire apprehension as well as awe. The spread of Chinese firms around the globe is no different. However, Chinese foreign direct investment (FDI) in the United States is not only small, but unusually small compared with what might be expected in the future. It is not too early to investigate what the data already show about Chinese FDI in the United States before examining the specific question of when foreign investment—especially foreign investment through acquisition of existing US firms—might pose a national security threat to the United States, and when national security concerns are not plausible.

Outward FDI from less developed and emerging-market economies—from China and others—has been increasing in recent years. China's outward FDI stock in 2010 was $298 billion, about two-thirds as much as Russia, 1.6 times as much as Brazil, and three times as much as India. And while China's outward FDI stock grew by almost 1,000 percent from 2000 to 2010, starting at a baseline of $28 billion, this is nothing compared with the growth rates of FDI from Russia and India, which increased by 2,000 and 5,200 percent over that same time period, starting from baselines of $20 billion and $1.7 billion, respectively. China's outward FDI flows so far place it far below the United States and other Organization for Economic Cooperation and Development (OECD) countries, far above most less developed countries, and in a broad middle range along with Russia, Brazil, and India. As our analysis delves deeper into the causes and consequences of Chinese FDI in the United States, unique characteristics of China and its FDI patterns will be discussed. But it is useful to keep in mind that at least in overall magnitude, Chinese outward FDI occupies the same middle range of a few other large emerging-market economies.

Empirical Issues Related to the Study of Chinese FDI

One difficulty that arises when trying to understand the effect of Chinese FDI in the United States is the lack of comprehensive and current data. There is no single data source that provides detailed real-time information on every aspect of Chinese investment. Data from official government sources take time to collect and compile. Private sources, such as Thomson and Dealogic, provide up-to-date information on individual companies investing in the United States, but problems arise in attempting to aggregate this information. However, there are several useful sources of data. Each has its own weaknesses, but taken together, they can paint a reasonably accurate picture of the state of Chinese FDI in the United States.

Chinese Ministry of Commerce

The Chinese Ministry of Commerce (MOFCOM) reports inward and outward FDI statistics, though a number of China experts have questioned the reliability of its data. Daniel Rosen and Thilo Hanemann (2009, 3) say that "although authorities conform in principle to internationally recognized standards, including the OECD's *Benchmark Definition of Foreign Direct Investment* and the International Monetary Fund's (IMF) *Balance of Payments Manual*, compilation methods are not fully consistent with these standards in practice, and MOFCOM's exact methodology for gathering OFDI [outward FDI] data is opaque." Kevin Cai (1999) reports that from the beginning of China's open door policy to the late 1990s, China's outward FDI flows are estimated by most sources to be between $80 billion and $100 billion, whereas the official statistics report only $15 billion.

United Nations Conference on Trade and Development (UNCTAD)

UNCTAD provides a more reliable picture of FDI stocks and flows using data that the IMF has collected from individual countries. These data are harmonized to allow for comparisons across countries and over time; however, the harmonization is not perfect due to idiosyncratic differences in the ways that individual countries define and measure FDI. In addition, the data are available only at an aggregate level, so they report the total outward FDI from China, but not the amount of that total investment that goes to the United States. This obviously limits their usefulness for understanding Chinese direct investment in the United States.

US Bureau of Economic Analysis (BEA)

The BEA collects firm-level data on affiliates of foreign-owned firms operating in the United States in its annual surveys of FDI. Responding to these surveys is mandatory for all firms located in the United States that have at least a 10 percent foreign ownership share and are above a minimum size threshold.

While firm-level data are not publicly available, the BEA does publish aggregate statistics by country of ownership and industry. These data include many useful balance of payments, financial, and operating statistics such as FDI position, capital inflows, sales, imports, exports, employment, wages, value added, and research and development (R&D) spending. One drawback is that the process of collecting, compiling, and verifying survey data means that they are not immediately available for analysis.

Rhodium Group's China Investment Monitor

Daniel Rosen and Thilo Hanemann of the Rhodium Group and the Peterson Institute for International Economics have recently developed a new dataset to track Chinese FDI in the United States called China Investment Monitor. This dataset compiles information on publicly announced acquisitions and greenfield investment by Chinese-owned firms using commercial databases such as Thomson, Dealogic, International Strategy and Investment (ISI), and fDi Markets, as well as news reports and their personal contacts in China. The greatest benefit of this dataset is that it allows for real-time analysis and is the most up-to-date source of information on Chinese FDI in the United States. However, because it records deals as they are announced, it may not pick up changes in the value or timing of expenditures associated with these deals that occur after the initial announcement. The China Investment Monitor only includes investments made since 2003 and thus does not allow for examination of longer-term trends. The focus on China also does not allow for easy comparisons with investments originating in other countries.

Heritage Foundation's China Global Investment Tracker

The Heritage Foundation also takes a deal-by-deal approach to tracking Chinese investment in its China Global Investment Tracker. This database contains details on over 400 attempted transactions, both successful and failed, by Chinese firms. It includes activities all over the world, not just in the United States, that occurred between 2005 and 2010 and involved over $100 million in value. This dataset allows for international comparison, but covers a relatively short time period and misses small-value transactions. Perhaps the greatest drawback is that the dataset attempts to capture all types of investment, not only FDI. Thus it combines portfolio flows with FDI data and necessarily misses a great deal of these flows, which are very difficult to track.

What Do the Data Say about Chinese Firms Operating in the United States?

To assess the effect of Chinese FDI in the United States, it is useful to first understand what form that investment takes. Figures 3.1 and 3.2 contain summary statistics on the characteristics of Chinese-owned firms in the

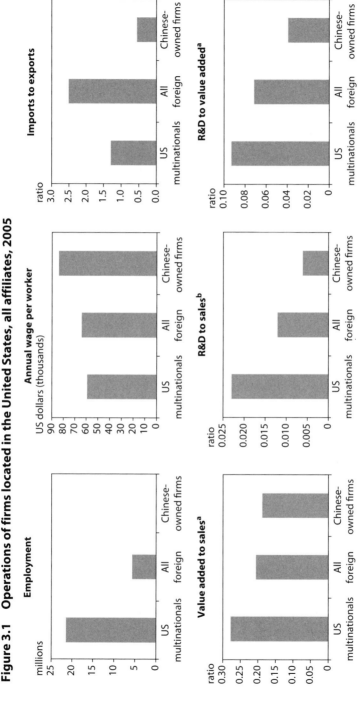

Figure 3.1   Operations of firms located in the United States, all affiliates, 2005

Employment

Annual wage per worker

Imports to exports

Value added to sales[a]

R&D to sales[b]

R&D to value added[a]

a. Value-added figures are for 2001.
b. Chinese sales and research and development (R&D) figures are for 2004.

Note: Chinese-owned firms are defined as firms for which a Chinese entity has at least 10 percent ownership.

Source: US Bureau of Economic Analysis.

Figure 3.2 Operations of firms located in the United States, majority-owned affiliates, 2007

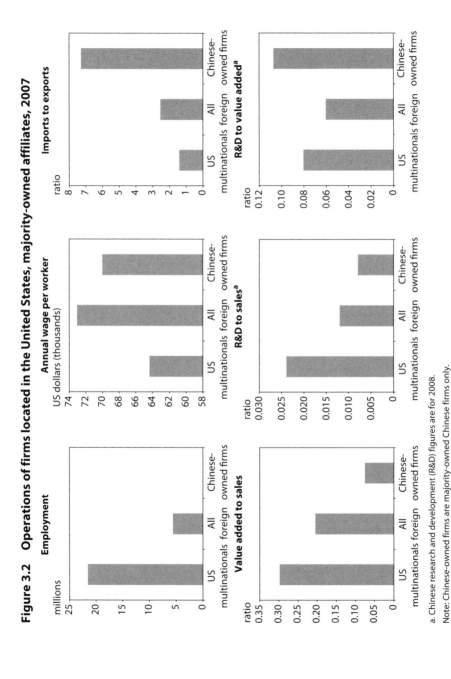

a. Chinese research and development (R&D) figures are for 2008.

Note: Chinese-owned firms are majority-owned Chinese firms only.

Source: US Bureau of Economic Analysis.

United States, comparing them with the same statistics for US-owned multinationals and other foreign-owned firms operating in the United States in 2005 and 2007. These data come from the BEA annual surveys of FDI in the United States.

Two different ownership thresholds typically are used to measure FDI activity. The first, which applies the standard definition of FDI used for balance-of-payments accounting, treats any domestic company that is at least 10 percent owned by a single foreign investor as a foreign-owned affiliate. The second, which is more commonly used in analyzing multinational company operations, focuses on companies that are majority-owned by foreign direct investors. The availability of data based on these alternative ownership thresholds varies, especially for China and countries like it, which have a relatively small amount of direct investment in the United States. For this reason, the figures in this chapter present data on Chinese FDI in the United States using both approaches.

The BEA does not report information on all measures of interest for all years. Because the data are collected directly from individual firms, to reveal too much detail in a year in which one large firm was particularly active would risk revealing confidential information about that firm. Thus the figures report data from the most recent years in which all key variables are available. When more recent information than that presented in the figures is available for certain measures, such as aggregate employment at Chinese firms in the United States, those more recent numbers are included in the text. Because Chinese FDI in the United States is still a relatively new phenomenon, the figures are simply meant to provide as much information as possible on the investments that have taken place so far and are not meant to precisely predict future trends, though some suggestions can be made.

Each graph in figure 3.1 shows the activities of all affiliates of foreign firms in the United States in the second bar and the activities of all Chinese-owned firms in the United States in the third bar, where foreign ownership is defined as occurring when a foreign resident has at least a 10 percent ownership stake in the affiliate. A limitation with these data, as mentioned above, is the relatively small amount of detail that the BEA has made public for recent years, given its increased emphasis on the data for majority-owned affiliates. Thus the most recent year for which data on most variables are available for Chinese-owned affiliates based on this broader definition is 2005. Figure 3.1 reports these data on the operations of all US affiliates of foreign firms, including Chinese firms, for 2005.

The second above-mentioned definition of FDI activity considers only affiliates in the United States for which a foreign firm controls a majority share. These data are presented in figure 3.2, using information from the BEA's most recent benchmark survey of direct investment in the United States, which covered FDI activity taking place in 2007.[1]

---

1. For a more in-depth discussion of the alternative definitions of FDI flows, see Lipsey (2001).

Chinese companies account for a very small share of both total US production and the total activities of all foreign firms operating in the United States. In 2005 broadly defined Chinese-owned firms employed only 2,400 workers in the United States, about 0.04 percent of all workers foreign firms employed in the United States in that year. By 2009 broadly defined Chinese-owned firms employed 5,000 to 10,000 US workers, about 1 to 2 percent of all US workers employed by foreign-owned firms and 0.004 to 0.007 percent of the total US labor force. Of these workers, in 2007, about 1,400 of them were employed by majority-owned affiliates of Chinese firms, as opposed to firms in which Chinese owners held a stake of only 10 percent or more. By 2009 this number was 4,300.

In the years for which comprehensive data are available, workers employed by firms with at least 10 percent Chinese ownership earned much higher wages than their counterparts at domestic or other foreign-owned firms. In 2005 the average annual wages and benefits US-owned multinationals paid to their US employees was about $60,000. The average for foreign firms operating in the United States was about $65,000. Chinese-owned firms paid their US employees significantly more than other firms, with average wages and benefits of about $85,000 per worker per year. The 2007 results for Chinese majority-owned firms are not quite as striking, as the wages they paid were higher than those of US-owned firms, but about the same as the wages paid by affiliates of firms headquartered in other foreign countries.

Why did companies with at least 10 percent Chinese ownership pay so much more than domestically owned firms and other foreign companies in 2005, and why did majority-owned Chinese affiliates pay so much more than domestic firms in 2007? The answer is not surprising in light of an assessment of why a Chinese firm would choose to operate in the United States in the first place. One of the primary motivations for FDI is to take advantage of differences across countries in wages, skill levels of workers, and other factors of production. US companies often move some or all of their production to less developed countries where low-skilled labor is abundant and thus production much less costly. However, it would not make sense for a Chinese company to move operations to the United States to hire low-skilled production workers, since these types of workers are much more abundant and receive much lower wages in China. Instead, Chinese companies locate in the United States to hire US workers to do what they do best: perform high-skilled activities, such as management and R&D. This is an important conceptual breakthrough. The instinct to rely on traditional motives for FDI, like relative wage rates or access to capital, clearly do not apply to nonextractive multinational corporations (MNCs) from emerging-market economies. Uphill FDI from poorer to richer countries is motivated by a desire to be near the global frontier in management and research and more affluent final consumers.

Another concern, as indicated earlier, is that foreign-owned firms may be more likely to source abroad than their domestically owned counterparts, which would negatively affect the US trade balance. This concern may be particularly acute for China, given the large trade deficit that the United States has with China in manufactured goods. Worry about the US-Chinese bilateral trade deficit as well as the overall US trade deficit arises with considerable regularity, but it is unclear why the level of imports on the part of foreign investors in the United States should be a part of it. As pointed out in chapter 1, the current account by definition is the difference between domestic savings and domestic investment, and FDI cannot affect the overall current account unless it somehow affects the demand for savings or investment. As long as the US government and private sector spend more than they earn, there will be no choice but to finance the difference with credit from abroad. However, given that critics of inward FDI often raise concern about the imports of foreign investors in the United States, it is worthwhile to explore the issue further.

What is striking about the evidence in figure 3.1 is that, unlike US multinationals and other foreign companies, firms with at least a 10 percent Chinese ownership share located in the United States actually export almost twice as much as they import. This suggests that Chinese firms are using their operations in the United States not only to serve US customers but also to export to customers in other countries, possibly even China itself. In this sense, this type of Chinese FDI in the United States may reduce the bilateral trade deficit between the United States and China. Thus, in addition to the role of FDI in substituting for imports described above, there could be a direct net positive trade balance effect of Chinese firms operating in the United States. However, the pattern only holds for firms with a 10 percent or greater Chinese ownership share in 2005, not for majority-owned Chinese firms in 2007. Also, import and export data for Chinese firms operating in the United States are not available for a very large number of years, so these flows may or may not indicate an enduring trend.

What can explain the different behaviors of affiliates of Chinese firms relative to those of other foreign firms, as well as the differences across years? One possible explanation is that Chinese multinationals operate in only a few main industries, and their behavior is consistent with firms of other nationalities operating in these industries. Chinese FDI activity in the United States is concentrated in chemicals and electrical equipment. If those industries pay higher wages and export more than others do, then some of the behavior of Chinese-owned firms in the United States could be explained by an industry composition effect. Figure 3.3 breaks down the summary statistics discussed above by sector. It does not report the breakdown of wages, employment, or trade for Chinese firms by industry. The BEA does not report all this information by detailed country and industry because there are so few Chinese firms operating in the United States in any given industry that revealing industry-level information on Chinese FDI risks revealing confidential information about individual firms. However, the data for US multinationals and aggregate totals for all other foreign firms confirm that in general, the industries that Chinese firms operate in most often do pay higher wages and have higher levels of exports relative to imports than the average for all industries, or even other manufacturing industries.

Figure 3.3   Operations of firms located in the United States, by sector, 2005

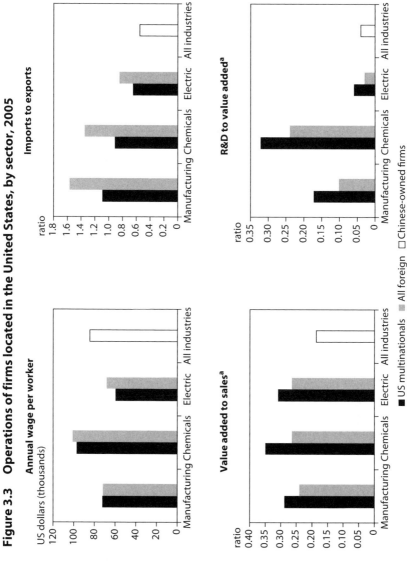

a. Value added figures are for 2001. Chinese sales and research and development (R&D) figures are for 2004.

Source: US Bureau of Economic Analysis.

Chinese firms in the United States spend less on R&D than US-owned firms do. However, this is to be expected of firms that are new to direct investment in the United States. R&D spending at US affiliates of Japanese firms was also very low in the early years of their FDI, but grew rapidly as Japanese investment in the United States grew (see figure 1.6 in chapter 1). As is discussed below, Chinese firms' R&D in the United States is already higher than that of firms headquartered in other emerging-market economies and can be expected to continue to grow.

Chinese FDI in the United States also differs from that of other firms in the BRIC countries (Brazil, Russia, India, and China). Figure 3.4 compares Chinese-owned firms with those headquartered in Brazil, India, and Russia. First, Chinese FDI in the United States is much smaller in magnitude than that from other BRIC countries, and Chinese firms in the United States employ a fraction of the number of workers employed by firms headquartered in other BRIC countries. This is surprising considering that China's total global outward FDI is larger than that of Brazil, Russia, or India. It suggests that investment in the United States is a much smaller share of total outbound FDI for China than for other emerging-market economies. This is likely because much of China's global FDI strategy focuses on natural resource extraction and thus targets Africa, Latin America, and other low-cost, resource-rich regions rather than the United States. However, Chinese companies operating in the United States pay higher wages than do Indian and Brazilian firms.

In addition to differences in magnitude, the data also suggest qualitative differences in the activities of Chinese-owned firms operating in the United States relative to firms based in other emerging-market economies. While Chinese R&D spending is lower than that of US multinationals and affiliates of other foreign firms in general, it is much higher than the R&D spending of other emerging-market firms operating in the United States. In 2007 Chinese firms spent $17 million on R&D at their US affiliates, while Brazilian, Indian, and Russian firms spent almost nothing. Even though Chinese direct investment in the United States is still relatively new, case study evidence suggests that the R&D spending of Chinese MNCs could be extremely large. Chinese telecommunications firm Huawei has invested in the United States in the past and has signaled a desire to continue doing so. According to Huawei's 2010 annual report, the firm has 20 research institutes globally, 46 percent of its employees are engaged in R&D activities, the annual research budget is $2.5 billion, and the firm has the largest number of patent applications in the world. The firm also claims to be a fierce defender of intellectual property rights around the world, as evidenced by its emphasis on patent applications. In 2010 Huawei reported employing 1,500 individuals in the United States, mostly engineers and managers working at labs and R&D facilities.

The Chinese appliance firm Haier similarly exemplifies the ramping up of R&D spending in the United States (box 3.1). According to business intelligence firm Euromonitor International, Haier is one of the top brands in the world for refrigeration and home laundry appliances. Haier first invested in

Figure 3.4   Employment, wages, and foreign trade of majority-owned affiliates of Chinese, Indian, Brazilian, and Russian firms operating in the United States, 2007

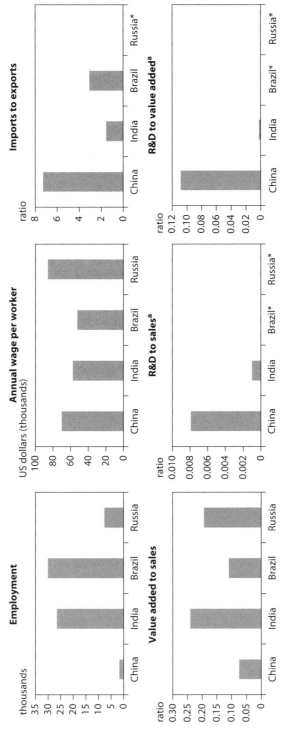

* = Suppressed to avoid disclosure of data on individual companies

a. Chinese research and development (R&D) figures are for 2008.

Source: US Bureau of Economic Analysis.

Box 3.1   Case study: Haier

Haier is a Chinese-owned appliance company with manufacturing operations in the United States, Europe, Asia, the Middle East, and Africa, and with R&D centers in the United States, Germany, Japan, and Korea. Haier had $20 billion in worldwide sales in 2010 and has sold over 40 million products in the Americas since 1999.

The evolution of Haier's US investments follows the expected pattern of FDI by emerging-market firms. As with many Japanese firms in earlier decades, Haier's initial US investments consisted of basic manufacturing, but over time the firm added increasingly higher-value activities, such as finance and engineering, to its US portfolio.

Timeline

1999: Haier America is founded with the development of a manufacturing facility in Camden, South Carolina.

2002: North American headquarters open in New York. Located in midtown Manhattan, the offices house executive staff. Administrative functions include branding, marketing, finance, and product innovations and engineering.

2004: New warehouse opens in Edison, New Jersey.

2005: Haier attempts to acquire Maytag but loses out to Whirlpool.

2006: Marketing partnership signed with the National Basketball Association.

US Locations

Headquarters: New York

Sales offices: Arkansas, California, Georgia, Iowa, Louisiana, Massachusetts, Miami, Mississippi, New Jersey, New York, North Carolina, Ohio, and Oregon

Factory: South Carolina

Warehouses: California, New Jersey, and South Carolina

Regional field service offices: Florida, Illinois, New York, and North Carolina

Source: Haier corporate website, www.haieramerica.com (accessed on December 13, 2012).

the United States in 1999 when it opened a manufacturing plant in Camden, South Carolina. That led to the opening of its US headquarters in New York City—which houses executive staff and administrative functions including branding, marketing, finance, product innovations, and engineering—and eventually to the opening of a design, research, and development center in Los Angeles. The Haier Group commits 5 percent of its revenue to R&D, which results in the company applying for hundreds of patents each year. The firm has eight R&D centers in the United States, Germany, Japan, and Korea. Chinese solar panel maker Suntech, which has its US headquarters in San Francisco, offers another example: Its R&D spending grew from $15 million in 2008 to over $40 million in 2010 (box 3.2).

The case study evidence, as well as the already relatively high level of Chinese firms' R&D spending in the United States, suggest that future growth in Chinese direct investment in the United States will be accompanied by increasing investment in R&D and other high value activities (see also box 3.3).

New Evidence on FDI Spillovers in the United States from Developing-Country Investment

Chapter 2 offers an updated assessment of spillovers from foreign investors to firms in the United States. This chapter expands that analysis to test for evidence of spillovers from less developed countries to US firms, using data for the years 1987 through 2007. As in chapter 2, the dependent variable in the analysis is firm-level total factor productivity (TFP) of US firms, which essentially captures how efficiently firms use a given set of inputs. TFP was computed using firm-level data from the Compustat database following the method in Olley and Pakes (1996), which allows for firm entry and exit and controls for the simultaneity of input choice and productivity. TFP, or how efficiently a firm i uses a given set of inputs at time t, is calculated as

$$tfp_{it} = y_{it} - \beta_k^{OP} k_{it} - \beta_l^{OP} l_{it} - \beta_m^{OP} m_{it} \qquad (3.1)$$

where y_{it} is the log of output and k_{it}, l_{it}, and m_{it} are the firm's log of capital, labor, and material inputs. β_k^{OP}, β_l^{OP}, and β_m^{OP} are the Olley-Pakes estimates of the capital, labor, and materials production function elasticities. Conceptually, this measure of TFP is simply the difference between the actual output of a firm and its expected output given the firm's capital, labor, and material inputs, where the expected effect of each input is calculated controlling for the endogeneity of productivity and input choice (as discussed earlier) as well as the possibility of firm exit. The effect of FDI on the productivity of US firms is estimated using the following equation:

$$\Delta tfp_{ijt} = \beta_0 + \beta_1 \Delta fdi_{jt-1} + \beta_2 \Delta fdi_{jt-2} + \sum_n \gamma_n X_{ijt} + \delta_j + \delta_t + \varepsilon_{ijt} \qquad (3.2)$$

The independent variable of interest, Δfdi, is the change in the share of employment at US affiliates of foreign firms in total US employment by industry and year. This measure of FDI employment shares is lagged by one and two years (denoted $t - 1$ and $t - 2$). Lagging the change in FDI share is important because it may take time for the spillover effects of FDI on

Box 3.2   Case study: Suntech

Suntech Power Holdings Co., Ltd. was founded in 2001 by Dr. Zhengrong Shi and is the largest supplier of solar panels worldwide. In 2010 over 15 million Suntech panels were installed in more than 80 countries. Suntech has offices in 13 countries, including regional headquarters in San Francisco, California; Schaffhausen, Switzerland; and Wuxi, China. Suntech has manufacturing sites in China, Japan, and the United States

Suntech is an example of a Chinese company that was attracted by the US research climate. Solar panel development relies heavily on R&D, so it is not surprising that Suntech chose to locate its US headquarters in the San Francisco Bay Area research hub. As the company expands, its investments in high-value activities in the United States are likely to grow as well. Suntech's R&D spending has already grown from $15 million in 2008 to over $40 million in 2010.

Timeline

2001: Suntech is founded by Dr. Zhengrong Shi in Wuxi, China.

2005: Initial public offering on the New York Stock Exchange.

2006: Suntech's direct investments in the United States begin.

2010: Suntech announces first US production line in Goodyear, Arizona.

US Locations

Regional headquarters: San Francisco

Manufacturing location: Goodyear, Arizona

Source: Suntech, *Suntech Power Holdings Co., Ltd. 2010 Corporate Report,* www.corporate-ir.net/Media_Files/IROL/19/192654/Suntech_2010_Corporate_Report.pdf (accessed on December 13, 2012).

---

domestic firms to materialize. Also, if FDI is attracted to industries in which firms exhibit the highest productivity growth, it is difficult to determine which direction the causality moves in: the presence of foreign firms leading to greater productivity among domestic firms or the existence of highly productive domestic firms attracting FDI. Including lagged variables helps sort this out by examining the effect of FDI in one year on the productivity of firms in that industry a year or two later. As mentioned in chapter 2, this method does not completely eliminate all potential endogeneity, as it assumes that firms cannot perfectly predict future productivity growth. However, it does remove at least some portion of the potential endogeneity. The regressions also control for a number of other factors, X_{ijt}, that will likely affect TFP changes, including the firm's capacity utilization, R&D spending, markups

---

Box 3.3   Case study: Wanxiang

Auto parts manufacturer Wanxiang Group Co., headquartered in Xiaoshan City, is China's second largest non-state-owned company.

Timeline

1994: US operations begin with the opening of Wanxiang America Corporation outside of Chicago.

1998: Partnership with Driveline Systems LLC.

2001: Acquires a 21 percent stake in Universal Automotive Industries Inc., a brake manufacturer.

2009: Receives a $2 million investment package from the state of Illinois to build a solar panel assembly plant in Rockford, Illinois.

2010: Employs 4,100 people in the United States.

US Locations

Regional headquarters: Elgin, Illinois. Responsible for engineering, logistics, quality assurance, marketing, and sales.

Source: Wanxiang America Corporation website, www.wanxiang.com (accessed on December 13, 2012).

---

above marginal cost, market share, and capital expenditures. Data on these firm-level characteristics are from Compustat. As explained in chapter 2, industry-level fixed effects are included to control for unobservable industry characteristics and year fixed effects are included to control for macroeconomic factors. These fixed effects control for everything that is constant, or fixed, about a given industry or year and thus affects all firms equally in that industry and at that time.

The results in table 3.1 offer very strong evidence of positive spillovers from direct investment in the United States—FDI from both developed countries and less developed countries such as China. The first column gives the results using FDI from all the countries presented in chapter 2. An increase in the share of US employment accounted for by foreign firms in a given industry is positively and significantly associated with growth in TFP, or how efficiently US firms use inputs in that industry. In other words, the presence of foreign firms makes domestic US firms more productive. The aggregate results, however, may mask important differences between the source countries providing the investment. It is not surprising that FDI from a highly developed country with firms producing cutting-edge technology spurs productivity growth among US firms. But does the same result hold for investment

Table 3.1 Spillover effects of a change in the industry-level FDI employment share on total factor productivity of domestic firms, by FDI source country

Variable	Model 1	Model 2	Model 3	Model 4
ΔFDI, $t-1$	80.53***	84.72***	−15.76**	33.01
	(30.28)	(30.56)	(6.19)	(74.63)
ΔFDI, $t-2$	274.59***	277.00***	15.14**	−23.75
	(29.67)	(29.92)	(5.95)	(73.09)
Capacity utilization	−0.21***	−0.21***	−0.28***	−0.29***
	(0.07)	(0.07)	(0.07)	(0.07)
Research and development	0.22***	0.22***	0.22***	0.22***
	(0.01)	(0.01)	(0.01)	(0.01)
Markup	6.09*	6.10*	5.94*	5.97*
	(3.19)	(3.19)	(3.20)	(3.20)
Market share	371.73***	372.05***	372.57***	373.07***
	(36.35)	(36.35)	(36.40)	(36.41)
Capx	−0.13***	−0.13***	−0.13***	−0.13***
	(0.003)	(0.003)	(0.003)	(0.003)
Industry fixed effects	yes	yes	yes	yes
Year fixed effects	yes	yes	yes	yes
R-squared	0.03	0.03	0.03	0.03
Number of observations	24,311	24,311	24,311	24,311
Dependent variable	Δtfp	Δtfp	Δtfp	Δtfp
Sample	All countries	High income	Low income	China

Notes: *, **, and *** indicate significance at the 10, 5, and 1 percent levels, respectively. Standard errors clustered by industry year are in parentheses.

Source: See text for the methods used to compute these results.

from developing countries such as China? Based on the results presented below, the answer is yes.

Column 2 of table 3.1 gives the results of the spillover analysis using only the share of total US employment accounted for by FDI from what the World Bank defines as high-income countries. These results are both qualitatively and quantitatively similar to the results using FDI from all countries, which is not surprising. Column 3 reports results using FDI from countries the World Bank classifies as low or middle income. These results show that productivity spillovers exist even when the investment is from a less developed country. For this type of FDI, the effect of foreign employment shares lagged one period is negatively associated with the productivity growth of domestic firms. However, the effect is positive after a two-year lag. This suggests that the spillover effects of FDI from low- to middle-income countries take longer to materialize than those of high-income countries. But there is every reason to expect positive spillover effects of FDI from all source countries, even those with incomes considerably less than the United States.

Column 4 considers only employment at affiliates of Chinese-owned firms. When the investigation is limited solely to FDI from China, the data show the presence of positive spillovers from Chinese investors, but the correlation is not statistically significant—that is, statistically strong enough to be certain that one will always find this outcome. This is not surprising because limiting the analysis to FDI from only one country necessarily reduces the statistical power of the results. The BEA collects FDI data through surveys of firms, which can then be aggregated up to the country and industry level. Examining only one country, especially one such as China, which has very little FDI in the United States, involves fewer firms in each industry, and thus any errors in reporting by a single firm will create more noise than aggregations using firms from a large number of countries. Looking at the results for the larger set of emerging-market economies presented in column 3 of table 3.1 actually provides better insights into the effect of Chinese FDI in the United States, and especially the potential future effect as Chinese FDI in the United States expands, due to the superior coverage of these data. The results indicate that FDI from China, like other emerging-market economies, will likely have positive spillover effects on the US economy.

The results should not be surprising. The spillover effects from manufacturing FDI into the United States from other developed countries are quite large, especially in US high-technology sectors, such as chemicals, computers and office equipment, electronic components, scientific instruments, and medical instruments. There is every reason to expect positive spillover effects from inward FDI from developing countries as well, including China—all the more so to the extent that such FDI takes place in high-tech sectors such as information technology and computers. That the earlier evidence shows Chinese FDI to be an outlier in undertaking R&D in the United States compared with other developing countries' FDI leads one to expect that spillovers from Chinese FDI to the US domestic economy will be disproportionately large in similar fashion.

Is There a High Level of Chinese FDI in the United States?

Whether or not there already is a high level of Chinese FDI in the United States might seem like a simple question that should be easy to answer by looking at the data. However, the reality is much more nuanced. Some high-profile cases of concern about Chinese FDI and US national security—analyzed in detail in chapter 4—may lead to the impression that Chinese FDI in the United States is already of large magnitude, as might instances in which US state or municipal governments tout the amounts of inward foreign investment and the numbers of jobs created in their communities. Yet analysts familiar with China's investment in other countries see Chinese direct investment in the United States as a small phenomenon relative to overall global activity. China's US FDI is also a small fraction of the FDI from more developed countries and even other emerging-market economies. Whether the volume of Chinese investment in the United States seems large or small depends on prior expectations about what that amount of investment should be.

A careful evaluation of the volume of Chinese FDI in the United States requires a framework for establishing some baseline expectation of FDI flows. One such framework is known as a gravity model. Gravity models were originally developed to explain trade flows between countries, but the principle has been shown to apply to FDI as well. The term *gravity* is borrowed from physics: Physical bodies are attracted to each other with a force proportional to their mass and distance from each other. The same is true of bilateral trade or FDI flows between countries, which are higher when the two countries are closer together and have larger GDPs. This finding is one of the strongest in empirical international economics and has been demonstrated repeatedly using a variety of datasets and time periods. When applied to a large dataset, the gravity model tells us the fundamental relation between factors such as GDP and trade. These fundamental relations then can be used to compare expectations based on country characteristics with actual levels of trade or FDI. If two countries are very close to each other geographically, or share a common border, one can expect large flows of trade and investment between them. If a country has a high GDP, one can expect that it will create a lot of products for export, consume a lot of imports, and be both a large recipient and a large provider of FDI. A common language also plays an important role. The gravity model puts numbers on the expected magnitude of these effects.

Table 3.2 presents the results for a simple gravity model of FDI. The numbers in the table represent the size of the relation between each variable and total FDI—say, how much FDI would be expected to increase or decrease with a change in GDP. These relations were estimated using data on FDI in the United States for about 50 countries over the years 1988 through 2007 from the BEA. The coefficient values for GDP, GDP per capita, and a variable indicating whether or not English is the official language of a given country are positive. This means that countries with higher GDP and GDP per capita, as well as countries that speak English, have a higher level of FDI in the United States, measured by both the total employment at US affiliates of firms headquartered in that country and the total sales of their US affiliates. The numbers in parentheses under the coefficient values are the standard errors of these estimates, indicating how confident one can be in their statistical significance. The errors are very small for all the variables, suggesting a high level of accuracy for the estimates.

The coefficient values for distance presented in table 3.2 are both negative, implying that greater distance from the United States is associated with lower volumes of both measures of FDI. The regressions were run in logarithms, which means that the coefficients can be interpreted as percentage changes. A 1 percent increase in the GDP of a country is associated with an increase in employment at US affiliates of firms from that country of 0.88 percent and results in affiliate sales that are about 1.1 percent higher. A 1 percent increase in GDP per capita leads to employment at US affiliates of firms from that country of 0.99 percent and results in 0.94 higher sales. A 1 percent increase in distance from the United States decreases FDI employment at firms from that country by 0.29 percent and decreases sales by 0.62 percent. Finally, countries where English is an official language have 290 percent higher employment at and 156 percent higher sales by their US affiliates than affiliates of firms from

Table 3.2   Determinants of employment and sales of US affiliates of foreign-owned firms

Variable	Employment	Sales
GDP	0.88***	1.10***
	(0.04)	(0.04)
GDP per capita	0.99***	0.94***
	(0.06)	(0.06)
Distance between countries	−0.29***	−0.62***
	(0.11)	(0.11)
English	1.36***	0.94***
	(0.16)	(0.17)
Number of observations	785	849
R-squared	0.67	0.65

Notes: *** indicates significance at the 1 percent level. Standard errors are in parentheses.

Source: See text for the methods used to compute these results.

non-English-speaking countries.[2] These relations are all very strong in both overall magnitude and statistical significance.

The gravity model creates a basis for what to expect would be normal levels of FDI from any given foreign country, so it is possible to use the coefficient estimates to predict the expected value of FDI employment and sales of Chinese firms in the United States for the years 1988 to 2007 and then compare the predicted values with the actual FDI levels. This comparison essentially captures how actual FDI by Chinese firms in the United States stacks up against what would be expected based on observations of the past behavior of firms from many countries with similar characteristics over many years. As shown in table 3.3, for all years of the sample, actual Chinese investment was about 50 percent lower than what the gravity model predicts. In 2007 there were 527,110 fewer Americans employed at Chinese firms operating in the United States than would be expected based on the characteristics of China's economy, location, and non-English-speaking society. These expectations are primarily driven by China's GDP. The results thus can be interpreted as saying that Chinese firms have done much less investing in the United States than one would expect from a country of its size, even when controlling for language, distance, and per capita income. How should one interpret the evidence that Chinese FDI in the United States is lower than that predicted by a simple gravity model? As mentioned, the extremely high predictions for Chinese FDI

---

2. The formula used to translate a dichotomous variable into an expected percentage increase is: $100*[\exp(b) - 1]$, where b is the coefficient estimate. Thus the additional percentages in employment and sales at foreign firms from English-speaking countries relative to those from non-English-speaking countries are $100*[\exp(1.36) - 1] = 290$ and $100*[\exp(0.94) - 1] = 156$, respectively.

Table 3.3   Actual versus predicted FDI from China, 1988–2007

Year	Actual – predicted employment (thousands)	Actual – predicted sales (thousands of US dollars)
1988	−8.33	−10,100
1989	−15.42	−12,800
1990	−4.77	−7,646
1991	−8.08	−8,863
1992	−21.36	−15,100
1993	−42.30	−24,700
1994	−33.30	−20,600
1995	−61.26	−33,000
1996	−82.57	−43,200
1997	−99.28	−50,500
1998	−109.93	−55,800
1999	−120.56	−60,800
2000	−139.87	−69,900
2001	−158.74	−78,800
2002	−181.64	−88,600
2003	−213.81	*
2004	−262.22	−125,000
2005	−318.51	*
2006	−395.86	*
2007	−527.11	*

* = Values for certain years are suppressed to avoid revealing confidential firm-level information.
Source: US Bureau of Economic Analysis.

in the United States are based primarily on China's GDP. The model leaves out some important factors. China differs in many ways from other countries with similar GDP levels, primarily in its history and the speed at which it achieved such a high level of income. Given China's ongoing emergence from a state-controlled communist economy, the comparatively weak record of Chinese FDI in the United States in past years is not surprising. Looking to the future, however, an appreciation of China's low levels of FDI in the United States acquires greater significance. The most plausible expectation is that Chinese FDI in the United States is likely to expand by large amounts. To further investigate this expectation, it is useful to consider other benchmarks as well.

Rosen and Hanemann Measures of Chinese FDI in the United States

Daniel Rosen and Thilo Hanemann of the Rhodium Group and the Peterson Institute for International Economics have compiled information on recent acquisitions and new investments by Chinese firms. They begin by looking at China's outbound FDI to all destinations in the world and point out that China's current FDI stock of $230 billion accounts for only 1.2 percent of the total global FDI stock, about the same as Denmark and slightly higher than Taiwan. China's outward FDI to GDP ratio is only 5 percent compared with a global average of 33 percent and a transitional economy average of 16 percent. However, given China's rapid growth and outward focus, Rosen and Hanemann

Figure 3.5   Chinese FDI stock by region, 2004–10

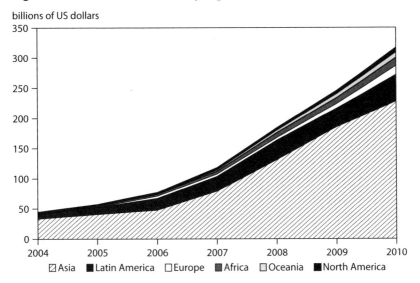

billions of US dollars

Asia   ■ Latin America   □ Europe   ■ Africa   □ Oceania   ■ North America

Source: Chinese Ministry of Commerce (MOFCOM).

project that China's total outward FDI will reach $1 trillion to $2 trillion by 2020 (Rosen and Hanemann 2011, 28).

Rosen and Hanemann also compile a new dataset of recent Chinese direct investments in the United States, called the China Investment Monitor. Based on these data, they conclude that "the Chinese FDI takeoff is under way, and Chinese investment in the United States is much greater than the official data suggest." From 2003 to 2007, the number of new Chinese FDI deals was roughly flat, with about 5 greenfield investments and 10 acquisitions per year. Rosen and Hanemann document a sharp upward trend after 2007, however: In 2010 Chinese FDI deals had increased to 25 greenfield projects and 34 acquisitions, together worth more than $5.4 billion and spanning a number of indus-tries. But unlike FDI in earlier years, most of the new investments since 2008 have taken place in manufacturing industries such as consumer electronics, machinery, auto parts, steel, and technology. Investment in higher value services such as finance is also expected to grow. Thus, Rosen and Hanemann's assertion about FDI takeoff by Chinese firms in the United States reinforces the gravity model's prediction in the preceding section.

How Does Chinese FDI in the United States Compare with Chinese FDI in Other Countries?

Another useful benchmark for examining Chinese FDI in the United States is to compare it with China's FDI in other countries. Chinese FDI in the United States has been increasing rapidly in recent years, but this pattern is not unique to the United States: China's total global outward FDI has been increasing as well, and the US share of total Chinese direct investment is not very large, as

Figure 3.6   US share in China's total outward FDI stock, 2004–10

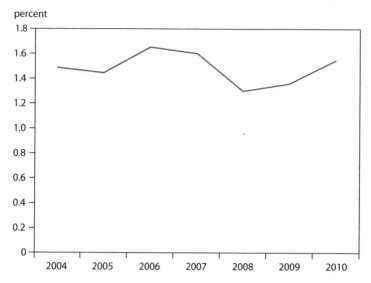

Source: Chinese Ministry of Commerce (MOFCOM).

figure 3.5 shows. The vast majority of Chinese outward FDI goes to other countries in Asia, and all other regions, including Europe, Latin America, and Oceania (primarily Australia and New Zealand), receive more Chinese direct investment than the United States does.

Figure 3.6 looks at the US share in total Chinese outward FDI. While total Chinese direct investment in the United States appears to be increasing rapidly in terms of pure dollar values, as a share of total Chinese investment, the United States remains a relatively tiny recipient. The share has fluctuated somewhat, but has remained at about 1.5 percent of total Chinese outward FDI. Much of China's outward FDI has focused on natural resource extraction and has thus been focused more on resource-rich regions with low-cost labor, such as Africa and Latin America, explaining at least part of the FDI pattern. Also, the data used to construct the figures are from MOFCOM and have a few shortcomings. They exclude financial sector investments and likely overstate the importance of Asia as a destination for Chinese FDI: Many investments ultimately destined for other locations first pass through Hong Kong, including some round tripping for investment back in China, and it is impossible to separate out the exact dollar value of these circuitous investments. However, even with these caveats, the data suggest very strongly that, in dollar values, Chinese FDI in the United States is a small drop in a very large bucket. This and the above analyses illustrate that levels of Chinese FDI in the United States are extremely low relative to a number of different benchmarks—though the trend for Chinese FDI in the United States is likely to turn upward sharply in the future.

FDI and National Security: Separating Legitimate Threats from Implausible Apprehensions

Foreign direct investment (FDI) that takes place through acquisition of an existing company in the home economy has long been a subject of particular sensitivity around the world, with frequent allegations that the outcome might negatively affect the national security of the home country. But what kind of acquisition would constitute a credible threat to national security? When would adverse national security consequences be implausible?

The US experience since the initial attachment of the Exon-Florio provision to the Omnibus Trade Act of 1988 shows that perceived threats to national security from foreign acquisition of a US company fall into three distinct categories.[1] The first category of threat (Threat I) is that the proposed acquisition would make the United States dependent on a foreign-controlled supplier for goods or services crucial to the functioning of the US economy—including, but not exclusively, the functioning of the defense industrial base—who could delay, deny, or place conditions on providing those goods or services. The second category of threat (Threat II) is that the proposed acquisition would allow transfer of technology or other expertise to a foreign-controlled entity that the entity or its government could deploy in a manner harmful to US national interests. The third category of threat (Threat III) is that the proposed acquisition would allow insertion of some capability for infiltration, surveillance, or sabotage—through a human or nonhuman agent—into the provision of goods or services crucial to the functioning of the US economy, including, but not exclusively, the functioning of the defense industrial base. The evolution of directives given to the Committee on Foreign Investment in the United States (CFIUS) from the Exon-Florio period through the latest Foreign Investment and National Security

---

1. This chapter draws on Moran (2009).

Act (FINSA) regulations has not, however, kept up with the understanding of what constitutes a potential threat to national security or appreciated the relatively rare circumstances in which such a threat might be credible.

Threat I: Denial or Manipulation of Access

The pressures that led to the original Exon-Florio provision in 1988 arose from a broad concern about the possible decline of US high-technology industries, aggravated by aggressive competition from Japan. From the rather shrill rhetoric about the Japanese threat, however, there emerged an increasingly sophisticated appreciation of what constituted genuine cause for alarm and what did not.

Fairchild Semiconductor

The immediate impetus for the passage of the Exon-Florio provision was the proposed sale of US company Fairchild Semiconductor by Schlumberger of France to Fujitsu in 1987. Commerce Secretary Malcolm Baldrige joined Defense Secretary Caspar Weinberger in arguing that the sale would give Japan control over a company that was a major supplier of chips to the US military. Other US semiconductor firms joined the argument against making US defense industries dependent on outsiders for high-technology inputs, and Fujitsu withdrew its bid for Fairchild. Shortly thereafter National Semiconductor acquired Fairchild at a substantial discount from the Japanese acquisition price, setting a precedent for the China National Offshore Oil Corporation (CNOOC)–Unocal case in 2005. Allegations about threats to national security can become a convenient vehicle for competitors to advance their own takeover plans and have to be evaluated independently and rigorously on the merits.

The criticism of the proposed acquisition rested on the premise that the target firm was in an industry crucial to the US economy and to US defense, with "crucial" defined in a commonsense manner that there would be a large negative effect if the economy had to do without the goods and services in question. There was no careful analysis of the conditions under which supply could be manipulated or withheld, or whether foreign corporate or government efforts to manipulate or withhold supply would have any practical effect. This changed in 1989 with the battle over a proposal by Nikon, a Japanese company, to acquire US company Perkin-Elmer's stepper division.

Perkin-Elmer

Steppers are advanced lithography equipment used to imprint circuit patterns on silicon wafers in the semiconductor industry. At the time of the proposed acquisition, Nikon controlled roughly half the global market for optical lithography and Canon, also a Japanese company, controlled another fifth (Bergsten and Noland 1993). If the acquisition were allowed, US producers would be highly constrained in where they could purchase machinery to etch microcircuits on semiconductors. The sale would effectively place quasi-monopoly power in the hands of the new owner, and by extension, the new owner's home government. Under the glare of scrutiny and political concerns, the acquisition did not proceed. The novel insight from the Perkin-Elmer case was that the term "crucial"—namely, the cost of doing without—had to be joined with parallel considerations: that there be a credible likelihood that a good or service could be withheld at great cost to the economy, or that the suppliers or their home governments could place conditions upon the provision of the good or service, which meant that the industry had to be tightly concentrated, the number of close substitutes limited, and the switching costs high.

The debate about Japanese company Nippon Sanso's proposal to acquire US firm Semi-Gas Systems in 1990 incorporated even more formally a methodology based on concentration of suppliers. The CFIUS process originally approved the sale of Semi-Gas by Hercules, its US parent company. But the US Department of Justice pointed out that the acquisition would raise the new Japanese owner's share of the global market to 40 percent, and therefore the Department of Justice would lodge an antitrust challenge to the proposed sale. The degree of market concentration raised not just the possibility of monopolistic pricing but the specter of other forms of discrimination in sales behavior. Once again US semiconductor firms, as well as Sematech, the Pentagon-supported industry consortium with the objective of boosting the competitiveness of the US computer chip manufacturing industry, were justifiably wary of finding themselves at the mercy of a foreign supplier of the specialized cabinets that store and distribute toxic gases used to make chips.[2]

Senator Lloyd Bentsen held hearings at which US semiconductor firms asserted that Japanese firms were disadvantaging US equipment users by withholding or delaying sales of state-of-the-art technology. A 1991 US General Accounting Office (GAO 1991) report did not uncover convincing support for these assertions or for other illegal or predatory behavior on the part of Japanese suppliers. But concerns about the Japanese government instructing US subsidiaries of home-country companies to behave in ways inimical to US national interests was not without foundation: Japan's Ministry of International Trade and Industry (MITI), under pressure from Socialist members of the Diet, did force Dexel, the American subsidiary of Japanese firm Kyocera, to withhold advanced ceramic technology from the US Tomahawk cruise missile program.[3]

---

2. The 2000 case of ASML of the Netherlands acquiring Silicon Valley Group to create the world's largest maker of semiconductor lithography equipment posed the same analytic problem. In this case, however, prominent US industry figures including Craig Barrett, CEO of Intel, lobbied in favor of the acquisition. The dilemma lay between becoming dependent on a quasi-monopolistic foreign supplier and relying on a less capable (and perhaps failing) national producer.

3. National Security Takeovers and Technology Preservation, Hearings before the Subcommittee on Commerce, Consumer Protection, and Competitiveness of the Committee on Energy and Commerce, House of Representatives, February 26 and June 12, 1991, 179.

Oregon Steel

The recognition that a proposed acquisition taking place in an industry identified as crucial was insufficient justification to block the acquisition emerged even more clearly in the case of a Russian oligarch's proposal to acquire Oregon Steel. In this case "crucial" was sometimes replaced with "critical," with the same implication of a high cost to the national economy if supply were manipulated or withheld. Would the acquisition of Oregon Steel in 2006 by the Russian company Evraz, which had close ties to Roman Abramovich, a Russian billionaire who enjoyed intimate relations with the Kremlin, pose a national security threat to the United States?

Following the methodology outlined above, for a foreign acquisition to pose a threat of the United States becoming dangerously dependent on a foreign supplier, CFIUS strategists have to evaluate both whether the good or service foreigners provide is crucial to the functioning of the US economy, including but not limited to its military services, and whether there is a credible likelihood that the good or service can be withheld—or that the suppliers, or their home governments, could place conditions on providing the good or service. The first evaluation clearly raises concerns: Steel is a major component of more than 4,000 kinds of military equipment, from warships, tanks, and artillery to components and subassemblies of myriad defense systems. Uninterrupted access to steel is likewise crucial for the everyday functioning of the US civilian economy. But the second evaluation dispels those concerns: In the international steel industry, the top four exporting countries account for no more than 40 percent of the global steel trade. Alternative sources of supply are widely dispersed, with 10 countries exporting more than 10 million metric tons[4] and 20 additional suppliers exporting more than 5 million metric tons.

The steel industry is vital to US national economic and security interests. But the multiplication of sources of supply around the world means that there is no realistic likelihood that an external supplier, or group of suppliers, could withhold steel from US purchasers or place conditions on US purchasers or the US government before delivery. The globalization of steel production allows US users to take advantage of the most efficient and lowest-cost sources of supply without a nagging worry that somehow the United States is becoming too dependent on foreigners. Evraz acquired Oregon Steel in 2006. The analytics applied in the Oregon Steel case could just as easily apply in assessing China's Angang Steel Company's proposed $175 million investment in 2010 to acquire a 20 percent stake in a rebar plant being built by a US company, Steel Development Company, in Amory, Mississippi—from which Angang backed away in the face of pressure from US lawmakers.

---

4. The 10 countries are Japan, Russia, Ukraine, Germany, Belgium-Luxembourg, France, South Korea, Brazil, Italy, and Turkey.

Threat II: Leakage of Sensitive Technology or Know-How

In almost all proposed acquisitions, it would be odd if the takeover did not offer the foreign parent corporation some new production or managerial expertise, giving the home government of the foreign parent an opportunity to command that the expertise be deployed in ways the home government desired. It would be equally odd if the additional production or managerial expertise did not, in some marginal way, strengthen the home government's national defense capabilities, including its military. Thus the second test interacts with the first. How broadly available is the additional production or managerial expertise involved? How big a difference would the acquisition make for the new home government?

LTV Missile Business

The prototypical illustration of potentially worrisome technology transfer can be found in the landmark case of the proposed 1992 acquisition of US company Ling-Temco-Vought's (LTV) missile business by Thomson-CSF of France.[5] The LTV Corporation found itself in bankruptcy due to underfunded pension obligations associated with the parent company's steel-making operations. To raise cash, a federal bankruptcy court in New York considered proposals from Martin Marietta, Lockheed, and Thomson-CSF to purchase LTV's missile division and approved sale to Thomson. Some of LTV's missile division capabilities were sufficiently close to those of multiple alternative suppliers that Thomson-CSF could obtain them elsewhere with relative ease. However, three product lines—the Multiple Launch Rocket System (MLRS) launcher, the Army Tactical Missile System (ATACM) longer-range rocket launcher, and the Line-of-Sight Anti-Tank (LOSAT) missile—had few or no comparable substitutes, and one—the Extended Range Interceptor (ERINT) antitactical missile—included highly classified technology that was at least a generation ahead of rival systems and virtually unique at the time. It is unclear from public sources exactly which LTV missile division products and services were formally included in the US export-control regime of the time.

Thomson-CSF was 58 percent owned by the French government, and in any case had a long history of closely following French government directives. The potential for sovereign conflict over the disposition and timing of Thomson-CSF sales, should the LTV missile division become part of the group, was substantial. Prior Thomson-CSF sales to Libya and Iraq had already provoked considerable controversy: a Thomson-built Crotale missile had shot down the sole US plane lost in the 1986 US bombing raid on Tripoli and Thomson radar had offered Iraq advance warning in the first Gulf War.

---

5. Materials prepared by Theodore H. Moran for the Subcommittee on Defense Industry and Technology, Senate Armed Services Committee, April 30, 1992.

The Department of Defense (DOD) initially informed Congress that the Pentagon would insist upon a special security agreement (SSA), or blind trust, to perform the security work on LTV programs, an arrangement Thomson-CSF at first opposed but ultimately accepted. CFIUS rejected the proposed acquisition when Thomson and the Pentagon failed to reach agreement on how to ensure that sensitive US technology did not seep through in any way to the new French parent. Thus the methodology for determining whether a foreign acquisition might threaten to provide a channel for some unacceptable leakage of technology or other know-how follows the same path as already outlined. The key lies in calculating the concentration or dispersion of the particular capabilities that the acquired entity possesses. When the entity presides over some unique or very tightly held capabilities that could damage US national interests if deployed, the threat is genuine.

The above analytics are helpful in understanding Lenovo's proposal to acquire IBM's PC business and Huawei's proposal to take a stake in 3Com. They also play a subtle role in the evaluation of CNOOC's proposal to acquire Unocal.

Threat III: Infiltration, Espionage, and Disruption

The 2005 Dubai Ports World (DP World) case brought to the fore an additional concern, namely, that a foreign acquisition might provide a setting in which the new owner was less than vigilant in preventing hostile forces from infiltrating the operations of the acquired company, or might even be complicit in facilitating surveillance or sabotage. In 2005 DP World sought to acquire the Peninsular and Oriental Steam Navigation Company (P&O), a British firm. P&O's main assets were terminal facilities owned or leased in various ports around the world, including facilities at six US ports in Baltimore, Houston, Miami, New Orleans, Newark, and Philadelphia. CFIUS initially approved the acquisition, but the deal later fell through after considerable public political pressure from US lawmakers.

The issue was not whether foreign ownership of a given service provider (e.g., ports administration), infrastructure network (e.g., telecommunications), or facility (e.g., a petrochemical plant) might lead to the new owner or the owner's home government denying services, or whether sensitive technology or other management capabilities might be transferred to the new owner or the owner's home government. Instead, concerns focused on whether foreign ownership offered an increased likelihood that what Edward Graham and David Marchick (2006) have called a "fifth column" might be able to penetrate the newly foreign-owned structure. Foreign acquisition might afford the new owner's government a platform for clandestine observation or disruption.

In addition to rejecting a proposed acquisition, CFIUS may deal with Threat III–type cases through remediation utilized for foreign takeovers when classified technologies and materials are involved, such as a requirement to set separate compartmentalized divisions within the company where US citizenship and special security vetting are required. As part of the process that led to the first CFIUS approval, the Department of Homeland Security negotiated a letter of assurances with DP World, stipulating that Dubai Ports would operate all US facilities with US management, designate a corporate officer with DP World to serve as point of contact with DHS on all security matters, provide information to DHS whenever requested, and assist other US law enforcement agencies on any matters related to port security, including disclosing information as US agencies requested (Graham and Marchick 2006). But public outcry against DP World ownership was sufficiently great that this mitigation agreement was dismissed out of hand, and the parent company withdrew its offer. Concerns about infiltration, espionage, and possible disruption reemerge in Huawei's proposal to take an ownership stake in 3Com.

Applying the Three-Threat Prism to Proposed Chinese Acquisitions

Lenovo's Acquisition of IBM's PC Business

Did Lenovo's acquisition of IBM's PC business in 2005 pose a credible national security threat to the United States? Regarding Threat I (denial) and Threat II (leakage of sensitive technology), competition among personal computer producers is sufficiently intense that basic production technology is considered commoditized. More than a dozen producers compete for 50 percent of the PC market, with none showing a predominant edge for long. It is far-fetched to think that Lenovo's acquisition of IBM's PC business represented a leakage of sensitive technology or provided China with military-application or dual-use capabilities that were not readily available elsewhere. Nor could Lenovo manipulate access to PC supplies in any way that would matter, as purchasers could simply shift to Dell, Hewlett-Packard, or any one of a number of other sellers. As for Threat III (infiltration, espionage, and disruption), any purchasers who feared bugs or surveillance devices within Lenovo PCs could purchase computers from other suppliers in whom they had more confidence.

Angang Steel Proposed Acquisition of a Stake in Steel Development Company

As suggested earlier, the analytics of Angang Steel Company's proposed $175 million investment to acquire 20 percent ownership of Steel Development Company in Amory, Mississippi, is even more straightforward, even though the acquisition did not occur. As the Angang investment would create a new company, not acquire a share in an established one, CFIUS would not have jurisdiction. But the threat framework is nonetheless useful. Steel is most certainly critical to the US economy and the US defense industrial base. But sources of supply are highly competitive and switching costs are low, so Threat

I is not worrisome. Rebar steel technology is commercially widespread, so Threat II does not apply. And a 20 percent ownership stake provides a poor platform for Threat III's preoccupation with sabotage. In the end, it was not careful threat assessment that led investors to abandon the project, but public uproar, including from established US steel companies for which the project would constitute a modern low-cost competitor.[6]

CNOOC's Proposed Acquisition of Unocal

The three threat assessment tools provide for a rigorous analysis of CNOOC's proposed acquisition of US oil company Unocal in 2005, which the Chinese company withdrew after substantial US political pressure. Looking solely at the question of whether oil is crucial for the functioning of the US economy and military, the answer is clearly yes. For many, this meant the case was closed.[7] From an analytical perspective, however, much was left to be considered, such as the concentration of alternative suppliers and potential switching costs, as well as potential leakage of sensitive technologies and managerial expertise.

In 2004 Unocal produced 159,000 barrels of oil per day (70,000 barrels per day in the United States) and 1.51 billion cubic feet of gas per day (577 million cubic feet per day in the United States); 33 percent of its oil and natural gas production was within the United States and 67 percent outside. Unocal had proven reserves of 659 million barrels of oil and 6.658 trillion cubic feet of natural gas. Of these reserves, 26 percent were within the United States and 74 percent outside. Concern was expressed that CNOOC might divert Unocal's energy supplies exclusively to meet Chinese needs. In the extreme, critics feared that CNOOC might reroute Unocal's US production back to China. This would be a highly complicated and expensive undertaking, as US pipelines across western states flow west to east; oil from the Gulf of Mexico would have to be shipped by tanker through the Panama Canal. But if it were accomplished, would this outcome harm the United States?

The diversion would constitute a threat to US interests only if sources of supply were tightly concentrated and switching costs high. But 21 countries—15 of them not members of the Organization of Petroleum Exporting Countries (OPEC)—have oil for export greater than Unocal's entire US production. Six more could be called upon to make up for a large fraction of Unocal's US output. With US oil consumption at 20.7 million barrels per day in 2005, and US oil imports at 12.4 million barrels per day, US buyers would simply replace Unocal's minuscule production—three-tenths of 1 percent of US use—with extra imports, leaving net imports and US balance of payments in

---

6. Compare Congressional Steel Caucus, letter to Secretary Timothy Geithner, July 2, 2010 with Stan Abram, "The Curious Case of Anshan Steel and the Space-Age Rebar Technology," *Forbes*, July 7, 2010.

7. Press statements on CNOOC's proposed acquisition of Unocal by Representative Joe Barton (R-TX) and Representative Duncan Hunter (R-CA).

energy unchanged. US courts could force CNOOC to pay the switching costs if contracts were broken.

It is commonplace to conclude that the United States needs an energy policy that promotes efficiency, reduces energy consumption, and stimulates the development of new energy sources that do not pollute or contribute to global warming. But the idea that policy toward CNOOC's acquisition would have affected US national energy interests, negatively or positively, does not survive rigorous scrutiny.

Protection of US interests derives from the dispersed structure and fungible qualities of the international oil industry. US oil from the Gulf of Mexico could be used to provision the Chinese People's Liberation Army (PLA) if the US government did not legally or physically block such shipments. But this would penalize the PLA by forcing it to buy expensive oil from North America compared with purchasing it from commercial suppliers closer to home. If CFIUS strategists could be permitted to enjoy a slyly mischievous sense of humor, CFIUS might have required a CNOOC-owned Unocal to ship all its North American output back to supply Chinese military forces. Moreover, in a bilateral crisis, perhaps over a confrontation across the Taiwan Strait, a CNOOC-owned US-based Unocal would be a hostage in US hands, not the other way around. Allowing Unocal business (and Lenovo-IBM business) to proceed as usual would be a bargaining chip for the US government to play, helping to offset countervailing Chinese pressures over US investors on the Chinese mainland.

Might the sale of Unocal to CNOOC have represented a leakage or loss of technology that could damage the United States (Threat II)? Looking strictly at oil production technology—possible enhancement of Chinese anti-submarine warfare (ASW) capabilities is considered below—the answer is no. If incorporating Unocal's technology and managerial expertise into CNOOC would have enhanced the latter's performance in discovering and producing oil, the result would have eased pressure on world energy markets. The spread of Unocal expertise throughout CNOOC would likely have had a small but positive global supply effect. If Unocal engineers and managers had improved CNOOC performance more than they might improve Chevron performance—Chevron ultimately acquired Unocal after CNOOC withdrew—the result would have been a net benefit for US and global energy consumers. On the demand side, the Chinese thirst for oil is a challenge that the entire world has to cope with. On the supply side, the Chinese drive to develop new energy sources is part of the solution, not part of the problem.[8] What serves US national interests can be illustrated with a hypothetical question: If China's government came to the World Bank for loans to support $1 billion of Chinese investments in prospective oil production, would US national interests be served by having the US

---

8. For an empirical assessment of whether Chinese investments are "locking up" world natural resources, or—in contrast—are serving to diversify and make more competitive the world natural resource base, see Moran (2010).

executive director vote yes or no? The answer is clearly yes, as it would help ease global production constraints.

But a complete assessment of CNOOC's proposed acquisition of Unocal requires a second pass through the questions of excessive dependence and potential leakage of technology. The question of excessive dependence arises because the Unocal purchase would have included a wholly owned subsidiary, Molycorp, that operates the only rare-earth mine located in the United States, at Mountain Pass, California. All US government stocks of rare earths in the National Defense Stockpile were sold off in 1998. In 2003 Molycorp ceased mining production at Mountain Pass, but the property remained open on a care-and-maintenance basis. Rare-earth supplies have become a matter of concern since 2009 as China has restricted exports and manipulated supply to show displeasure in foreign policy disputes with Japan. A thorough CFIUS analysis today would consider whether Molycorp should be included in the proposed CNOOC acquisition of Unocal or sold off to an American buyer separately.

Regarding potential leakage of sensitive technology, assertions were made that Unocal seismic technology had dual-use possibilities, reinforcing Chinese ASW capabilities as well as enhancing oil exploration. Investigating these assertions would involve highly specialized, and perhaps highly classified, expertise. Once again, however, the algorithm to be followed would take the form of what has been laid out above: Would acquiring Unocal's seismic technology confer capabilities that are closely held and not available for purchase or hire by China from other alternative sources?

Huawei, Bain Capital, and 3Com[9]

In late 2007 Bain Capital proposed to acquire 3Com, a leading US hardware and software network company based near Boston, for $2.2 billion, with 16.5 percent minority shareholding by Huawei, including the right to appoint 3 of 11 board members.[10] Huawei was founded in 1988 by a former Chinese army officer, Ren Zhengfei. In 2005 the Rand Corporation reported that Huawei had ties with the Chinese government, in particular the People's Liberation Army (PLA) (Medeiros et al. 2005). The DOD 2008 annual report to Congress on the military power of the People's Republic of China named Huawei, along with Datang and Zhongxing, as working with the PLA on techniques of cyber warfare. 3Com had already formed a joint venture with Huawei in China, referred to as H3C, which the 3Com parent subsequently bought out to incorporate into its production chain as a wholly owned affiliate. For its part, Huawei had larger market penetration in Europe than in the

---

9. For detailed background on Huawei, see Barfield (2011).

10. 3Com Corporation, Proxy Statement Pursuant to Section 14(a) of the Securities Exchange Act of 1934. Washington, DC: United States Securities and Exchange Commission, January 24, 2008.

United States and could use a stake in 3Com to provide channels into the US market quite independent of any interest in 3Com products or services.

The *Washington Times* leaked news that CFIUS had serious national security concerns about the proposed acquisition, provoking criticism about violations of confidentiality on CFIUS submissions.[11] How might this acquisition have posed a national security risk to the United States? This case provides particular insight into the interaction between Threats II and III. The roster of 3Com products suggested as many as nine clusters of goods and services that might be considered crucial to the functioning of the US economy and defense industrial base and that might provide important capabilities to the Chinese economy and defense industrial base, including routers, switches, interface cards, and—most important—network security systems. These needed to be subjected to the concentration-level and switching-cost tests discussed above.

Addressing Threat I first, could the Bain purchase, with the Huawei minority stake, lead to circumstances—perhaps during a US-China crisis—in which critical 3Com capabilities were withheld from US users? On its face, it would appear implausible that a Huawei minority interest would be enough to allow Chinese interests, or the Chinese government, to dictate how 3Com goods and services were offered for sale in the market. A large fraction of 3Com products are assembled in the wholly owned H3C affiliate and shipped from China; China could embargo them, along with other output that companies such as Cisco or Ericsson produce or assemble on the mainland. But the Huawei ownership share in 3Com would not per se enhance the options available to the Chinese government one way or another.

Turning to Threat II, would the Bain purchase, with the Huawei minority stake, allow the leakage of sensitive technology or other capabilities to Chinese users that they would not otherwise have access to? The CFIUS threat assessment would likely have discerned for each of the nine 3Com clusters whether alternative suppliers were few enough, and switching costs high enough, that the acquisition offered a nonreproducible channel to obtain the technology or other capabilities. A survey of public sources indicates that most of the router, switch, and internet card capabilities of 3Com products are rather widely available commercially for Chinese use, many involving hardware and software already produced in China. A focus of particular attention, however, was 3Com's prize-winning integrated security and intrusion-protection system, called Tipping Point, that featured US government and military agencies among its purchasers. Tipping Point is built around an application-specific integrated circuit (ASIC)–based engine that performs thousands of high-speed checks on each data packet the recipient receives.

How concentrated is the international market for a Tipping Point–like threat suppression engine? A review of commercial sources suggests at least 12 US players in this market, including Cisco Systems, Juniper Networks, Sourcefire, IBM, McAfee, Top Layer Networks, Radware, NFR Security, Reflex

---

11. Bill Gertz, "Intelligence Report Hits China Deal," *Washington Times,* November 30, 2007, A1.

Security, DeepNines, Still Secure, and NitroSecurity, plus European and Asian firms. Specialized expertise would be required to compare the individual attributes of these alternative security systems, but it would appear that Chinese agencies have redundant access to capabilities similar to those of Tipping Point. After some initial reluctance, 3Com and Bain announced that they were prepared to spin off the Tipping Point operations.

Regarding Threat III, the 3Com case introduced an apprehension that has plagued Huawei ever since: that the acquisition might allow for infiltration, surveillance, or sabotage of 3Com's goods and services—or, as a special case of Threat III, that the proposed acquisition might provide insight into weak points of a system that even purchasers and users, including the US government, might not be fully aware of. On March 19, 2008, Bain announced that it was withdrawing its proposal to acquire 3Com. Two years later Hewlett Packard bought 3Com and began to see products in the United States from 3Com's Chinese facilities, an observation that will receive more detailed analysis later in this chapter.

In 2010 Huawei purchased the patent portfolio of 3Leaf, a near-bankrupt Silicon Valley company that had no other bidder on its assets, and hired some of its staff. Only after it discovered CFIUS was investigating the acquisition did Huawei file official notice. Two months later CFIUS informed Huawei that it would recommend to the president that the company divest itself of all 3Leaf assets. In reaction, Huawei issued an open letter defending its reputation and inviting US government agencies to investigate the company. In the end, the company accepted the divestiture, agreeing to appoint an officer whose responsibility was to show US agencies periodically that the company was in compliance.

Apprehension about infiltration, surveillance, and sabotage via Huawei information technology (IT) goods and services extends beyond acquisitions of US companies over which CFIUS has jurisdiction. Huawei was a leading bidder on an AT&T plan to upgrade the US network to operate with 4G technology in 2009, only to find that the head of the National Security Agency (NSA) told AT&T that Huawei must be excluded from consideration if AT&T wanted to maintain its government contracts. In 2010, as Huawei appeared set to win major network upgrade business from Spring Nextel, the secretary of commerce placed a personal call to Sprint's CEO to warn that Sprint's relationship with government agencies would be imperiled if it chose Huawei as a service provider. The instinct to exclude Chinese companies extends beyond mergers and acquisitions over which CFIUS has authority to government contracts, private contracts, joint ventures, and R&D partnerships.

In an attempt to assuage ongoing concerns about Threat III—whether through acquisition of a company or through commercial provision of goods and services—Huawei has established a security assurance program in which the company offers all source code in escrow to a trusted third party that can verify that goods and services are clean to buyers or governments. The most advanced instance of such vetting is Huawei's Cyber Security Evaluation Center at Basingstoke in the United Kingdom, staffed by Huawei employees who are UK nationals with UK government security clearances. Forensic audits of Huawei hardware and software take place according to UK government parameters and the results are shared with UK intelligence and other agencies, which are expected to share information with counterparts in the United States, Australia, Canada, and elsewhere. Complementing this audit of hardware and software is the proposal that indigenous trusted third-party installers, such as Bechtel, CDTI, or TESSCO, take goods and services that have been verified as secure and deliver, install, maintain, and manage upgrades and updates for purchasers. No Huawei individual or entity thus touches Huawei goods or services between the security audit and the installation or upgrade with final users.

The security assurance arrangement may provide a model that extends far beyond concerns about foreign acquisitions of local companies. As cybersecurity experts such as James Mulvenon and James Lewis point out, global supply chains that supply IT infrastructure are pervasive, containing hardware and software that come from China, Russia, Malaysia, Mexico, and Eastern Europe.[12] Cisco, Ericsson, Lucent-Alcatel, Samsung, and other international IT firms source goods and software from Chinese facilities staffed by Chinese engineers often within sight of Huawei facilities. Scott Charney, corporate vice president of trustworthy computing at Microsoft, argues that cyber security cannot be achieved by trying to single out firms of a particular nationality or firms with production in a particular country (Charney 2008). On the second Tuesday of each month, he reports, Microsoft applies patches and upgrades to many millions of computers in China, including those of the PLA. "China and other governments have expressed concerns about back doors in US products," notes Charney.[13] "When asked about this, I have stated numerous times that Microsoft does not put back doors into its products. Indeed, if we did, it would undoubtedly be discovered and then we would be out of business." National and international efforts to deal with cyber intrusion will have to address purchases of hardware, software, installations, upgrades, and patches from providers of all nationalities operating from all locations. Protection from threats may require an array of independent cyber security cells around the globe that vet the hardware and software of all major IT providers, providing assessments to private clients and governments alike—a vast subject well beyond the scope of this volume.

Tightening CFIUS Appraisal of Potential National Security Threats from Proposed Foreign Acquisitions

Each of the three threats described above can be found in the language of Section 721 of the Defense Production Act of 1950 and subsequent amendments,

---

12. This cyber-security appraisal draws upon Barfield (2011).

13. Personal communication on December 18, 2011.

including FINSA.[14] But the language fails to adequately guide an analysis to identify realistic national security threats or set aside implausible national security preoccupations.

Concern about Threat I (denial) is expressed, among other places, in consideration of whether the acquisition "could result in control of a person engaged in interstate commerce in the United States by a foreign government or an entity controlled by or acting on behalf of a foreign government."[15] But the concept of control is not operationalized to mean that the acquirer could delay, deny, or place conditions upon providing a good or service to adversely affect US national security. For this to be possible, as argued above, the number of suppliers must be concentrated, the number of close substitutes limited, and switching costs high. Otherwise Lenovo's purchase of IBM's computer business might be considered a shift of control to China—true enough—even as Lenovo's PCs are so generic that hypothetical Chinese government instructions to withhold PC sales to US buyers would have no perceptible effect on US national security.

Concern about Threat II (leakage) is expressed, among other places, in consideration of the potential effects of the transaction on transfer of military capabilities: "the potential effects of the transaction on sales of military goods, equipment, or technology."[16] But the worry about leakage is not qualified by consideration of whether alternative sources of military goods, equipment, or technology are readily available to a country or not. When sources of supply are so diverse that there are off-the-shelf commercial substitutes for the goods and services that a target of foreign acquisition provides, there is no basis for determining that an acquisition might open a channel for leakage of goods, equipment, or technology.

Concern about Threat III (sabotage, espionage) is expressed, among other places, insofar as "the term 'national security' shall be construed so as to include those issues related to 'homeland security,' including its application to critical infrastructure.... The term 'critical infrastructure' means...systems and assets, whether physical or virtual, so vital to the United States that the incapacity or destruction of such systems or assets would have a debilitating impact on national security."[17] As argued earlier, CFIUS-FINSA language might be amplified to include infiltration and surveillance, plus detection of network weaknesses and possible internal system manipulation. But the broader issue for the United States and other states worried about cyber security is how to protect against potentially infected goods and services by screening them

---

14. US Department of the Treasury, Committee on Foreign Investment in the United States (CFIUS), Section 721 of the Defense Production Act of 1950, Final Regulations, Issued November 14, 2008, www.treas.gov (accessed on October 30, 2011).

15. FINSA, Section 2, (a), (3), (4).

16. Section 721 (f) of the Defense Production Act of 1950.

17. FINSA, Section 2, (a), (5), (6).

wherever they come from and through whatever channel they are purchased, a challenge in which foreign acquisitions per se are only a subset.

CFIUS members and staff, intelligence community support, and Congressional overseers should generally be able to find adequate justification in current legislation and regulations to deal with the three threats identified here. But they are left without appropriate filters to discern truly troublesome cases from harmless ones. Much more problematic for the review process, the legal language involving "critical" and "essential" are introduced without qualification, leaving great potential for protectionist mischief. For example, "the term 'critical technologies' means critical technology, critical components, or critical technology items essential to national defense."[18] Foreign acquisition of a US steel producer, as in the Oregon steel case, would certainly involve a "critical" and "essential" item of importance to national defense, leading the reader of FINSA, Section 2, (a), (7) possibly to consider the acquisition a national security threat. There is no guidance to point out that the multiplicity and diversity of alternative steel suppliers would render any attempt to delay, deny, or place conditions on access of supply to be entirely useless, and any transfer of technology to be inconsequential. This omission is likely to doom debate about foreign acquisitions in the United States, like debate about foreign acquisitions in other countries, to assertions that every "critical" or "essential" sector be kept in the hands of home-country citizens.

The approach recommended here for CFIUS assessments can readily be generalized for multilateral use among developed and developing states. Looking first at more developed countries, the Three Threats framework fits comfortably within the Guidelines for Recipient Country Investment Policies Relating to National Security, a set of recommendations the Organization for Economic Cooperation and Development (OECD) Council adopted in May 2009, while suggesting a decision tree for OECD members to evaluate the plausibility of actual national security threats. The utility of the framework does not rely on agreement among the community of nations as to which countries might be considered "good" or "bad" states (or "hostile" or "rogue" or "unreliable"). Rather, the framework is constructed with a realpolitik assessment that governments have different and sometimes seriously conflicting conceptions of their own national interests, allowing national authorities to ponder carefully whether a foreign acquisition credibly poses any of the three threats identified here. The fundamental value of the framework is to separate plausible from implausible threats in a manner that all nations might commonly accept. That is, individual states could base their own behavior around the framework, recognizing that they can live comfortably within a global regime in which others behave in a similar fashion.

When is blocking foreign acquisitions pure protectionism? The framework offered here does not attempt to second-guess the specific motives for any given rejection of a proposed foreign acquisition; rather, the intention is to offer a

---

18. FINSA, Section 2, (a), (7).

rigorous line of reasoning to identify credible threats. There will always be close calls along the margin. But US experience suggests that public officials need a decision tree to help them determine when high-profile contentions are simply bogus, often fueled at least in part by acquisition-minded US competitors.

The framework introduced here complements and enhances the goals of transparency of policies, predictability of outcomes, measures of general application that treat similarly situated investors in a similar fashion, proportionality of measures, and accountability of implementing authorities as set forth in OECD guidelines for recipient country investment related to national security. It advances the guidelines' purposes in two ways. First, the OECD guidelines permit that "essential security concerns are self-judging"; that is, "OECD investment instruments recognize that each country has a right to determine what is necessary to protect its national security." The decision tree in figure 4.1 offers a common path for all OECD members to evaluate whether concerns about a possible national security threat are plausible. Second, the OECD Investment Committee occasionally uses the term "strategic industries" in ways that suggest entire sectors—energy, military suppliers, financial institutions, infrastructure—might be excluded from foreign takeovers. The threat assessment tool developed here allows for finer discrimination as to when a proposed foreign acquisition might pose a threat.

Use of the decision tree need not be limited to OECD members. It can equally well form the basis for non-OECD nations, such as Brazil, Russia, India, or China. In assessing the degree of competition among suppliers and switching costs, it is important to focus on the global market, not the domestic market; the relevant measurement is whether an acquisition increases the concentration in the global market to a worrisome extent, not whether the acquired firm is the last producer on home-country soil. There will be many instances in which a foreign company may acquire the last remaining national producer of a given good or service, but the international market is sufficiently competitive that it makes no substantive difference for the home country's national security.

Can a quantitative standard be used to guide an OECD-wide, or world-wide, plausible threat test—that is, to determine whether there are "widely available substitutes for goods and services of the target acquired firm in global markets, competitive suppliers in global markets, [and] low switching costs"? The most obvious tool to operationalize the degree of competition among suppliers is to use the long-standing US Department of Justice and Federal Trade Commission—or similar EU Directorate General for Competition—guidelines on mergers and acquisitions.[19] The goal is not to turn the national

19. US Department of Justice/Federal Trade Commission, "Commentary on the Horizontal Merger Guidelines," March 2006, www.usdoj.gov/atr/public/guidelines/215247.htm (accessed on December 20, 2012); European Union, European Commission's Directorate-General for Competition (EU DG Competition), January 2008, http://ec.europa.eu/atoz_en.htm (accessed on December 20, 2012).

Figure 4.1 Decision tree to assess national security rationale for blocking foreign acquisition

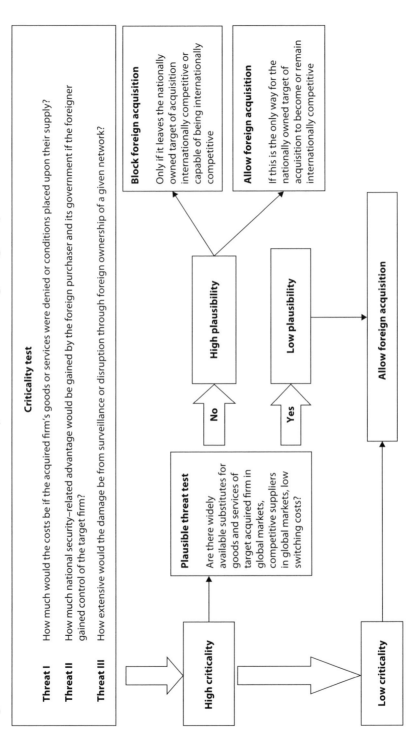

Criticality test

Threat I How much would the costs be if the acquired firm's goods or services were denied or conditions placed upon their supply?

Threat II How much national security–related advantage would be gained by the foreign purchaser and its government if the foreigner gained control of the target firm?

Threat III How extensive would the damage be from surveillance or disruption through foreign ownership of a given network?

Block foreign acquisition

Only if it leaves the nationally owned target of acquisition internationally competitive or capable of being internationally competitive

Allow foreign acquisition

If this is the only way for the nationally owned target of acquisition to become or remain internationally competitive

High plausibility

Low plausibility

Plausible threat test

Are there widely available substitutes for goods and services of target acquired firm in global markets, competitive suppliers in global markets, low switching costs?

High criticality

Low criticality

No

Yes

Allow foreign acquisition

security framework into an antitrust issue, but to limit national security scrutiny to circumstances in which denial of access to an acquired firm's goods or services would impose high costs, or in which the unwanted advantage to the foreign purchaser and its government would be large, or in which damage from surveillance or disruption through foreign ownership of a supplier would be unavoidable. In each case, national security monitors would want to look for consequences that affected the home country in ways far beyond raising prices.

5

Policy Implications: Making the United States More Accessible to Foreign Investors

The preceding analysis shows that foreign multinational firms that invest in the United States are, alongside US-headquartered American multinationals, the most productive and highest-paying segment of the US economy. They conduct more research and development (R&D), provide more value added to US domestic inputs, and export more goods and services than other firms in the US economy. The superior technology and management techniques they employ spill over horizontally and vertically to improve the performances of local firms and workers. Their corporate social responsibility activities provide tangible benefits to the communities where they locate their plants and research facilities. As the United States wants not only to expand employment but also create well-paying jobs that reverse the falling earnings that many US workers and middle class families have suffered in recent decades, it is more important than ever to enhance the United States as a destination for multinational investors.

Multinational corporations (MNCs) target the United States for investment overwhelmingly because the US economy gives them access to skilled and energetic workers. The US workforce today is willing to work more hours at (often) multiple jobs than ever before. But after more than a century of spectacular progress, in recent years the rate of US educational advance has sharply decelerated. From 1940 to 1980 the mean educational attainment of all US workers climbed by 0.86 years per decade, from 9.01 to 12.46 years, but from 1980 to 2005 the total increase was no more than one year—only 0.43 years per decade (Kirkegaard 2007, Goldin and Katz 2008, Baily and Slaughter 2008). This slowdown in education has taken place while improvements in secondary education have accelerated around the world. Other countries have not merely been catching up to the US workforce; they have been moving ahead.

Among 26 member states of the Organization for Economic Cooperation and Development (OECD) in 2006, 18 had high school graduation rates higher than that of the United States. At the same time there have been concerns about the quality of US education, with US students scoring below the median in comparative tests of educational achievement in science and mathematics. Maintaining the competitive quality of the US labor force is a dynamic process. As Jacob Kirkegaard points out, the retirement of the baby-boom generation in the United States represents the largest brain drain, or skill drain, that has ever taken place from any economy in history, and replacement indicators are not promising (Kirkegaard 2007). Measures to improve the education and skill level of the US workforce are therefore vital to making the United States an ongoing attractive site for international investment.

A particularly important component of improving the human capital resources within the US labor market is policy toward high-skilled immigration. Immigrants with college or higher degrees bring skills directly into the US labor pool, as well as innovative ideas for new goods and services and connections to business networks in their home countries. Approximately one-quarter of all US high-technology startups since the early 1990s have had at least one foreign-born cofounder, up from less than 10 percent in the 1970s (Kirkegaard 2007). But the US H-1B visa program places stringent caps on the inflow of engineers, scientists, architects, doctors, and managers from abroad. As a result, the most competitive companies in the United States—including US affiliates of foreign multinationals—cannot get visas for the non-US high-skilled workers they want to hire. A snapshot from 2008 shows that about half of 163,000 companies in the United States wishing to hire a foreign high-skilled worker on H-1B visas were denied this opportunity by the annual quota of 85,000 available permits.[1] For a more recent illustration, any US firm that wanted to hire a foreign-born high-skilled person in December 2011 had to wait until April 1, 2012, as that fiscal year's quota had already been filled.[2] Reforming US policy toward high-skilled immigration would make the US economy more competitive as a site for US and non-US investors alike. Strengthening the quality and size of the skilled labor force in the United States through both education and immigration policies will increase the appeal of the United States as a location for high-value production, attracting investment that will utilize this larger pool of indigenous and foreign-born workers while benefiting the overall US economy.

State-of-the-art infrastructure—ports, airports, railroads, roads, bridges, tunnels, information technology, and electrical grids—is likewise crucial for MNCs to manage worldwide production and coordinate international supply chains. While alternative host-country sites around the world are upgrading

---

1. Jacob Funk Kirkegaard, "US High-Skilled Immigration Policy: A Self-Inflicted Wound," *YaleGlobal Online*, July 1, 2008.

2. US Citizenship and Immigration Services, "USCIS Reaches Fiscal Year 2012 H-1B Cap," press release, November 23, 2011, www.uscis.gov (accessed on December 11, 2012).

their infrastructure in clearly visible ways, the United States is falling behind in both relative and absolute terms (Deshpande and Elmendorf 2008). US spending on public infrastructure has declined on a gross and net basis. The American Society of Civil Engineers awarded a grade of D to the quality of US infrastructure in its *2009 Report Card for America's Infrastructure*.[3] It graded 15 segments of US infrastructure, from aviation to transit and wastewater, and found delayed maintenance and chronic underfunding as contributors to poor outcomes.

The US tax system is particularly business-unfriendly for foreign companies considering the United States as a site for business (Hufbauer and Wong 2011). The US statutory corporate tax rate (federal and state combined) is the second highest, behind Japan, among OECD countries. At 39 percent, the combined US tax rate is 11 percentage points higher than the unweighted average of competing countries. However, it is not only statutory rates that make the United States unfriendly to businesses. The US average effective tax rate, again combining federal and state, is also second highest. The US marginal effective corporate tax rate may take the prize for highest. Gary Hufbauer concludes that the United States has just about the "worst corporate tax system from the standpoint of encouraging investment in plant and equipment (P&E) or research and development (R&D), or promoting production for home or export markets."[4]

The payoff from lowering the US tax rate and simplifying the US tax code would be substantial (Hufbauer and Wong 2011). Econometric estimates suggest that cutting the corporate tax rate by 1 percentage point would, over time, increase the output produced by foreign firms operating in the United States by at least 2 percent. Cutting the US corporate tax rate by 10 percentage points could potentially increase their employment by 1 million more Americans, above the 56 million Americans foreigners currently employ.

On June 20, 2011, President Obama issued a major statement reiterating the US commitment to welcome investment from abroad. But to many observers, the United States is becoming less open and even protectionist toward inward investment. Most foreign MNCs establish a presence in the US economy through mergers and acquisitions: Of approximately $2 trillion in inward investment between 1987 and 2006, 88.8 percent took place by foreign companies acquiring existing US businesses, rather than by greenfield investment to establish a completely new business (CFR 2011, footnote 95). The tendency of some foreign acquisition cases—in particular, Dubai Ports World and the China National Offshore Oil Corporation (CNOOC)—to become highly politicized, however, may give external investors pause in considering this route. Adherence to the framework for the Committee on Foreign

---

3. American Society of Civil Engineers, *2009 Report Card for America's Infrastructure*, www. infrastructurereportcard.org (accessed on December 11, 2012).

4. Gary Clyde Hufbauer, US Corporate Tax Reform, Testimony before the Hearing on Tax Reform and Foreign Investment in the United States, US House of Representatives Committee on Ways and Means Subcommittee on Select Revenue Measures, June 23, 2011.

Investment in the United States (CFIUS) decision making that separates genuine national security threats from spurious allegations (see chapter 4) would adequately protect the United States while tamping down political interference in the acquisition process.

Finally, the United States might want to undertake new initiatives to attract inward investment at the national level instead of leaving investment promotion activities almost entirely to the states. SelectUSA, the federal government initiative that has replaced Invest in America, is the closest program the United States has to a national investment promotion agency, but it is underfunded and understaffed. Lacking sufficient funding for large-scale outreach, SelectUSA currently functions primarily as a clearinghouse for information. Its website offers a searchable guide to federal programs and services available to businesses operating in the United States and a catalogue explaining the advantages of operating in the country. However, the information is sparse given the lack of federal initiatives on inward foreign direct investment (FDI). The site also includes links to individual states' economic development agencies, though as a federal agency, SelectUSA must remain neutral with respect to the states and cannot advise or consult with companies on which locations they should choose within the United States.

Looking specifically at the future of FDI from China in the United States, the outlook presented here—like that of other researchers, including Daniel Rosen and Thilo Hanemann—is that the types and amounts of Chinese FDI can be expected to grow rapidly, and that the benefits accruing to US firms, workers, and communities will likely expand rapidly as well. But this may not happen as rapidly as would be optimal for the United States. The evidence in chapter 3 shows that Chinese investors pay wages above the average for US or other foreign-owned firms, and contrary to some fears, Chinese companies in the United States are not mere vehicles for imports of Chinese goods. Rather, Chinese investors are attracted by the superior human capital they find in the United States—despite recent declines in educational standards—and they use their US plants as sources of US exports, so much so that in some years their exports of US-produced goods have been greater than their imports from other countries. Chinese firms also use the US economy as a base for conducting R&D, with expenditures as a proportion of value added higher than comparable US firms and significantly higher than other investors from developing countries. The capabilities Chinese investors bring to their US operations spill over and improve the efficiency of other firms in the US economy.

As much of Chinese FDI will take place through acquisition of existing US firms, US authorities will want to be vigilant in assessing the potential for threats to national security identified in chapter 4. But vigilant does not mean exclusionary. As with foreign investment from other sources—the Middle East, other Asian countries, Europe, Russia, and the developing world—the conditions within which foreign acquisition might pose a credible national security threat can be rigorously defined and assessed, allowing the vast majority of FDI acquisitions to pass through unimpeded.

In addition to economic benefits, there are strategic reasons to encourage Chinese FDI in the United States. The Chinese government has made the expansion of FDI by Chinese firms a top priority. From a strategic perspective, removing barriers and encouraging firms to invest gives the United States a strong bargaining chip in future interactions. Chinese ownership of US firms locates Chinese assets on US soil, under US jurisdiction, giving the United States greater leverage in its interactions with China. This principle applies to environmental and labor concerns as well as economic and security issues. Chinese firms in the United States must abide by US laws, including those relating to the environment and treatment of workers. Individuals concerned about the poor record of Chinese firms on these issues should want to encourage those firms to locate their production in the United States, as doing so will put them under tighter regulations and hold them to higher standards of conduct than if they produced the same output in China.

Chapter 3 shows that Chinese FDI in the United States is currently quite low in relation to a number of benchmarks. A standard predictive gravity model indicates that Chinese FDI is lower than what would be expected given China's GDP, population, and per capita income. Chinese FDI in the United States also has been growing more slowly than that of countries in a similar stage of development, including Brazil, Russia, and India. As outbound FDI from China continues to grow very rapidly, however, US policy should not focus on how to keep Chinese FDI out, but how to attract more Chinese direct investment into the US economy.

It is an understatement that information is far from perfect about Chinese perceptions regarding the potential for investing in the United States. The cultural and language barriers to be overcome are very high. Even factual comparisons are often far off the mark. John Ling, managing director of the South Carolina State Office in Shanghai, has found that many Chinese companies he speaks with about investing in South Carolina are shocked to learn how low the costs of doing business are in the United States.[5] Because the United States is among the most developed countries in the world, Chinese executives tend to think that everything must be more expensive than in China. When the Chinese owner of a plastics company asked what he would have to pay a manager if he opened a production facility in South Carolina, he was surprised by the answer—about $150,000 per year—as that was what the owner was currently paying his general manager in China. The Chinese plastics investor was also surprised to discover that the cost of electricity is about two to three times higher in China than it is in South Carolina, and that the supply of US electricity is much more reliable than it is in some regions in China, where his plants experienced frequent power outages. These are just a few examples of extremely widespread misperceptions among Chinese firms about the benefits of investing in the United States.

---

5. Oldenski interview, Shanghai, July 21, 2011.

There is a large role that SelectUSA or a similar agency could play at the federal level alongside vigorous state level representations to demonstrate the advantages of choosing the US economy as a site for Chinese firms to invest. As Chinese FDI increases, taking along Chinese managers from Chinese US affiliates as satisfied customers might go a long way to overcome cultural and language barriers. The message, however, must be unambiguous: Except for a very few rigorously defined national security exceptions, Chinese investment is welcome in the United States.

Overall, to the extent the United States can make the domestic economy a more attractive locale for international companies from all over the world to base their operations, US workers, firms, communities, and consumers will benefit.

References

Adler, Matthew, and Gary Clyde Hufbauer. 2008. *Policy Liberalization and FDI Growth, 1982 to 2006.* Working Paper 08-7. Washington: Peterson Institute for International Economics.

Anderson, Thomas. 2008. US Affiliates of Foreign Companies: Operations in 2006. *Survey of Current Business* 88, no. 8 (August): 186–203.

Anderson, Thomas, and William J. Zeile. 2009. Operations of US Affiliates of Foreign Companies: Preliminary Results from the 2007 Benchmark Survey. *Survey of Current Business* 89, no. 11 (November): 43–65.

Baily, Martin N., and Matthew J. Slaughter. 2008. *Strengthening US Competitiveness in the Global Economy.* Washington: Private Equity Council.

Barfield, Claude. 2011. *Telecoms and the Huawei Conundrum: Chinese Foreign Direct Investment in the United States.* Washington: American Enterprise Institute.

Bergsten, C. Fred, and Marcus Noland. 1993. *Reconcilable Differences? United States–Japan Economic Conflict.* Washington: Institute for International Economics.

Bernard, Andrew B., and J. Bradford Jensen. 1999. Exceptional Exporter Performance: Cause, Effect, or Both? *Journal of International Economics* 47, no. 1: 1–25.

Bernard, Andrew B., J. Bradford Jensen, and Peter K. Schott. 2005. *Importers, Exporters and Multinationals: A Portrait of Firms in the U.S. that Trade Goods.* NBER Working Paper no. 11404. Cambridge, MA: National Bureau of Economic Research.

Bernard, Andrew B., Jonathan Eaton, J. Bradford Jensen, and Samuel Kortum. 2003. Plants and Productivity in International Trade. *American Economic Review* 93: 1268–90.

Blalock, Garrick, and Paul J. Gertler. 2005. Foreign Direct Investment and Externalities: The Case for Public Intervention. In *Does Foreign Direct Investment Promote Development?* ed. Theodore H. Moran, Edward M. Graham, and Magnus Blomström. Washington: Institute for International Economics and Center for Global Development.

Blalock, Garrick, and Paul J. Gertler. 2008. Welfare Gains from Foreign Direct Investment Through Technology Transfer to Local Suppliers. *Journal of International Economics* 74, no. 2 (March): 402–21.

Blomström, Magnus. 1986. Foreign Investment and Productive Efficiency: The Case of Mexico. *Journal of Industrial Economics* 35, no. 1 (September): 97–100.

Blomström, Magnus, and Fredrik Sjöholm. 1999. Technology Transfer and Spillovers: Does Local Participation with Multinationals Matter? *European Economic Review* 43, no. 4-6: 915–23.

Bradford, Scott C., Paul E. Grieco, and Gary Clyde Hufbauer. 2005. The Payoff to America from Global Integration. In *The United States and the World Economy: Foreign Economic Policy for the Next Decade*, by C. Fred Bergsten and the Institute for International Economics. Washington: Institute for International Economics.

Brainard, S. Lael. 1993. *A Simple Theory of Multinational Corporations and Trade with a Tradeoff between Proximity and Concentration*. NBER Working Paper no. 4269. Cambridge, MA: National Bureau of Economic Research.

Brainard, S. Lael. 1997. An Empirical Assessment of the Proximity-Concentration Tradeoff Between Multinational Sales and Trade. *American Economic Review* 87, no. 4 (September): 520–44.

Branstetter, Lee. 2006. Is Foreign Direct Investment a Channel of Knowledge Spillovers? Evidence from Japan's FDI in the United States. *Journal of International Economics* 68, no. 2 (March): 325–44.

Cai, Kevin G. 1999. Outward Foreign Direct Investment: A Novel Dimension of China's Integration into the Regional and Global Economy. *China Quarterly* 160 (December): 856–80.

Capanelli, Giovanni. 1997. Buyer-Supplier Relations and Technology Transfer: Japanese Consumer Electronics. *International Review of Economics and Business* 44, no. 3: 633–62.

Carr, David L., James R. Markusen, and Keith E. Maskus. 2001. Estimating the Knowledge-Capital Model of the Multinational Enterprise. *American Economic Review* 91, no. 3 (June): 691–708.

CFR (Council on Foreign Relations). 2011. *US Trade and Investment Policy*. Independent Task Force Report no. 67. Andrew H. Card and Thomas A Daschle, chairs; Edward Alden and Matthew J. Slaughter, project directors. New York.

Charney, Scott. 2008. *Establishing End to End Trust*. Redmond, WA: Microsoft Corporation.

Chung, Wilbur, and Juan Alcacer. 2002. Knowledge Seeking and Location Choice of Foreign Direct Investment in the United States. *Management Science* 48, no. 12 (December): 1534–54.

Costinot, Arnaud, Lindsay Oldenski, and James Rauch. 2011. Adaptation and the Boundary of Multinational Firms. *Review of Economics and Statistics* 93, no. 1 (February): 298–308.

Deshpande, Manasi, and Douglas W. Elmendorf. 2008. *An Economic Strategy for Investing in America's Infrastructure*. Hamilton Project Strategy Paper. Washington: Brookings Institution.

Doms, Mark E., and J. Bradford Jensen. 1998. Comparing Wages, Skills, and Productivity Between Domestically and Foreign Owned Manufacturing Establishments in the United States. In *Geography and Ownership as Bases for Economic Accounting*, ed. Robert E. Baldwin, Robert E. Lipsey, and J. David Richardson. Washington: National Bureau of Economic Research and Chicago: University of Chicago Press.

Ekholm, Karolina, Rikard Forslid, and James R. Markusen. 2007. Export-Platform Foreign Direct Investment. *Journal of the European Economic Association* 5, no. 4: 776–95.

Feenstra, Robert C., and Gordon H. Hanson. 1997. Foreign Direct Investment and Relative Wages: Evidence from Mexico's Maquiladoras. *Journal of International Economics* 42, no. 3-4 (May): 371–93.

Feinberg, Susan E., and Michael P. Keane. 2005. Intrafirm Trade of US MNCs: Findings and Implications for Models and Politics Toward Trade and Investment. In *Does Foreign Direct Investment Promote Development?* ed. Theodore H. Moran, Edward M. Graham, and Magnus Blomström. Washington: Institute for International Economics and Center for Global Development.

Figlio, David N., and Bruce A. Blonigen. 2000. The Effects of Foreign Direct Investment on Local Communities. *Journal of Urban Economics* 48, no. 2 (September): 338–63.

GAO (US General Accounting Office). 1991. *US Business Access to Certain Foreign State-of-the-Art Technology* (September). Washington.

Glickman, Norman J., and Douglas P. Woodward. 1991. Regional and Local Determinants of Foreign Firm Location in the United States. In *Industry Location and Public Policy,* ed. Henry W. Herzog and Alan M. Schlottmann. Knoxville, TN: University of Tennessee Press.

Goldin, Claudia, and Larry Katz. 2008. *The Race Between Education and Technology.* Cambridge, MA: Harvard University Press.

Görg, Holger, and Eric Strobl. 2005. Spillovers from Foreign Firms Through Worker Mobility: An Empirical Investigation. *Scandinavian Journal of Economics* 107, no. 4 (December): 693–709.

Graham, Edward M., and Paul R. Krugman. 1995. *Foreign Direct Investment in the United States*, 3d ed. Washington: Institute for International Economics.

Graham, Edward M., and David M. Marchick. 2006. *US National Security and Foreign Direct Investment.* Washington: Institute for International Economics.

Haskel, Jonathan E., Sonia Pereira, and Matthew Slaughter. 2007. Does Inward FDI Boost the Productivity of Domestic Firms? *Review of Economics and Statistics* 89, no. 3 (August): 482–96.

Helpman, Elhanan. 1984. A Simple Theory of International Trade with Multinational Corporations. *Journal of Political Economy* 92, no. 3 (June): 451–71.

Helpman, Elhanan, Marc Melitz, and Stephen Yeaple. 2004. Export Versus FDI with Heterogeneous Firms. *American Economic Review* 94, no. 1 (March): 300–316.

Horstmann, Ignatius J., and James R. Markusen. 1992. Endogenous Market Structures in International Trade. *Journal of International Economics* 32, no. 1-2 (February): 109–29.

Hufbauer, Gary Clyde, and Woan Foong Wong. 2011. *Corporate Tax Reform for a New Century.* Policy Briefs in International Economics 11-2. Washington: Peterson Institute for International Economics.

Hummels, David, Jun Ishii, and Kei-Mu Yi. 2001. The Nature and Growth of Vertical Specialization in World Trade. *Journal of International Economics* 54, no. 1 (June): 75–96.

Javorcik, Beata. 2004. Does Foreign Direct Investment Increase the Productivity of Domestic Firms? In Search of Spillovers through Backwards Linkages. *American Economic Review* 94, no. 3 (June): 605–27.

Javorcik, Beata, and Mariana Spatareanu. 2005. Disentangling FDI Spillover Effects: What Do Firm Perceptions Tell Us? In *Does Foreign Direct Investment Promote Development?* ed. Theodore H. Moran, Edward M. Graham, and Magnus Blomström. Washington: Institute for International Economics and Center for Global Development.

Katz, Jorge M., ed. 1987. *Technology Generation in Latin American Manufacturing Industries.* New York: St. Martin's Press.

Keller, Wolfgang, and Stephen R. Yeaple. 2009. Multinational Enterprises, International Trade, and Productivity Growth: Firm-Level Evidence from the United States. *Review of Economics and Statistics* 91, no. 4 (November): 821–31.

Kirkegaard, Jacob Funk. 2007. *The Accelerating Decline in America's High-Skilled Workforce: Implications for Immigration Policy.* Policy Analyses in International Economics 84. Washington: Peterson Institute for International Economics.

Kohpaiboon, Archanun. 2007. *Multinational Enterprises and Industrial Transformation: Evidence from Thailand.* Cheltenham, UK: Edward Elgar.

Kohpaiboon, Archanun. 2009. *Global Integration of the Thai Automotive Industry.* Thammasat University Discussion Paper 0016. Bangkok: Thammasat University.

Kokko, Ari. 1994. Technology, Market Characteristics, and Spillovers. *Journal of Development Economics* 43, no. 2 (April): 279–93.

Krugman, Paul. 1983. New Theories of Trade Among Industrial Countries. *American Economic Review* 73, no. 2 (May): 343–47.

Lipsey, Robert. 2001. *Foreign Direct Investment and the Operations of Multinational Firms: Concepts, History, and Data.* NBER Working Paper no. 8665. Cambridge, MA: National Bureau of Economic Research.

Markusen, James R. 1997. *Trade Versus Investment Liberalization.* NBER Working Paper no. 6231. Cambridge, MA: National Bureau of Economic Research.

McKendrick, David G., Richard F. Donner, and Stephan Haggard. 2000. *From Silicon Valley to Singapore: Location and Competitive Advantage in the Hard Disk Drive Industry.* Stanford, CA: Stanford University Press.

Medeiros, Evan S., Roger Cliff, Keith Crane, and James C. Mulvenon. 2005. *A New Direction for China's Defense Industry.* Santa Monica, CA: Rand.

Melitz, Marc J. 2003. The Impact of Trade on Intra-Industry Reallocations and Aggregate Industry Productivity. *Econometrica* 71: 1695–725.

Moran, Theodore H. 2009. *Three Threats: An Analytical Framework for the CFIUS Process.* Policy Analyses in International Economics 89. Washington: Peterson Institute for International Economics.

Moran, Theodore H. 2010. *China's Strategy to Secure Natural Resources: Risks, Dangers, and Opportunities.* Policy Analyses in International Economics 92 (July). Washington: Peterson Institute for International Economics.

Moran, Theodore H. 2011. *Foreign Direct Investment and Development: Launching a Second Generation of Policy Research, Avoiding the Mistakes of the First, Reevaluating Policies for Developed and Developing Countries.* Washington: Peterson Institute for International Economics.

Mrázová, M., and J. P. Neary. 2011. Firm Selection into Export-Platform Foreign Direct Investment. Unpublished paper (February).

OECD (Organization for Economic Cooperation and Development). 2011. Productivity Statistics. Paris. Available at www.oecd.org/std/productivitystatistics/productivitystatistics.htm.

Oldenski, Lindsay. 2012. The Task Composition of Offshoring by US Multinationals. *International Economics* 131, no. 3: 5–21.

Olley, S., and A. Pakes. 1996. The Dynamics of Productivity in the Telecommunications Equipment Industry. *Econometrica* 64, no. 6 (November): 1263–97.

Pack, Howard. 1997. The Role of Exports in Asian Development. In *Pathways to Growth: Comparing East Asia and Latin America*, ed. Nancy Birdsall and Fredrick Jaspersen. Baltimore: Johns Hopkins University Press.

Pavcnik, Nina. 2002. Trade Liberalization, Exit, and Productivity Improvements: Evidence from Chilean Plants. *Review of Economic Studies* 69: 245–76.

Ramachandran, V. 1993. Technology Transfer, Firm Ownership, and Investment in Human Capital. *Review of Economics and Statistics* 75, no. 4 (November): 664–70.

Rasiah, Rajah. 1995. *Foreign Capital and Industrialization in Malaysia.* New York: St Martin's Press.

Rhee, Yung Whee, Katharina Katterback, and Jeanette White. 1990. *Free Trade Zones in Export Strategies.* Washington: World Bank Industry Development Division.

Richardson, David, and David M. Huether. 2001. Imputing and Interpreting Trade in Intermediate Goods and Services: A U.S. Illustration for the 1990s. Manuscript.

Rosen, Daniel H., and Thilo Hanemann. 2009. *China's Changing Outbound Foreign Direct Investment Profile: Drivers and Policy Implications.* Policy Briefs in International Economics 09-14. Washington: Peterson Institute for International Economics.

Rosen, Daniel H., and Thilo Hanemann. 2011. *An American Open Door? Maximizing the Benefits of Chinese Foreign Direct Investment.* Special Report. Washington: Center on US-China Relations, Asia Society, and Kissinger Institute on China and the United States, Woodrow Wilson International Center for Scholars.

Simon, Herbert A. 1951. A Formal Theory of the Employment Relationship. *Econometrica* 19, no. 3 (July): 293–305.

Tadelis, Steven. 2002. Complexity, Flexibility, and the Make-or-Buy Decision. *American Economic Review Papers and Proceedings* 92, no. 2: 433–37.

Williamson, Oliver E. 1985. *The Economic Institutions of Capitalism: Firms, Markets, Relational Contracting.* New York: Free Press.

Verhoogen, Eric. 2007. *Trade, Quality Upgrading and Wage Inequality in the Mexican Manufacturing Sector: Theory and Evidence from an Exchange Rate Shock.* CEPR Discussion Paper 6385. London: Centre for Economic Policy Research.

Yeats, Alexander J. 2001. Just How Big Is Global Production Sharing? In *Fragmentation: New Production Patterns in the World Economy,* ed. Sven W. Arndt and Henryk Kierzkowski. Oxford: Oxford University Press.

Index

Other Publications from the
Peterson Institute for International Economics

WORKING PAPERS

Reconcilable Differences? United States-Japan Economic Conflict* C. Fred Bergsten and Marcus Noland
June 1993 ISBN 0-88132-129-X

Does Foreign Exchange Intervention Work? Kathryn M. Dominguez and Jeffrey A. Frankel
September 1993 ISBN 0-88132-104-4

Sizing Up U.S. Export Disincentives* J. David Richardson
September 1993 ISBN 0-88132-107-9

NAFTA: An Assessment Gary Clyde Hufbauer and Jeffrey J. Schott, *rev. ed.*
October 1993 ISBN 0-88132-199-0

Adjusting to Volatile Energy Prices Philip K. Verleger, Jr.
November 1993 ISBN 0-88132-069-2

The Political Economy of Policy Reform John Williamson, ed.
January 1994 ISBN 0-88132-195-8

Measuring the Costs of Protection in the United States Gary Clyde Hufbauer and Kimberly Ann Elliott
January 1994 ISBN 0-88132-108-7

The Dynamics of Korean Economic Development* Cho Soon
March 1994 ISBN 0-88132-162-1

Reviving the European Union* C. Randall Henning, Eduard Hochreiter, and Gary Clyde Hufbauer, eds.
April 1994 ISBN 0-88132-208-3

China in the World Economy Nicholas R. Lardy
April 1994 ISBN 0-88132-200-8

Greening the GATT: Trade, Environment, and the Future Daniel C. Esty
July 1994 ISBN 0-88132-205-9

Western Hemisphere Economic Integration* Gary Clyde Hufbauer and Jeffrey J. Schott
July 1994 ISBN 0-88132-159-1

Currencies and Politics in the United States, Germany, and Japan C. Randall Henning
September 1994 ISBN 0-88132-127-3

Estimating Equilibrium Exchange Rates John Williamson, ed.
September 1994 ISBN 0-88132-076-5

Managing the World Economy: Fifty Years after Bretton Woods Peter B. Kenen, ed.
September 1994 ISBN 0-88132-212-1

Reciprocity and Retaliation in U.S. Trade Policy Thomas O. Bayard and Kimberly Ann Elliott
September 1994 ISBN 0-88132-084-6

The Uruguay Round: An Assessment* Jeffrey J. Schott, assisted by Johanna Buurman
November 1994 ISBN 0-88132-206-7

Measuring the Costs of Protection in Japan* Yoko Sazanami, Shujiro Urata, and Hiroki Kawai
January 1995 ISBN 0-88132-211-3

Foreign Direct Investment in the United States, 3d ed. Edward M. Graham and Paul R. Krugman
January 1995 ISBN 0-88132-204-0

The Political Economy of Korea-United States Cooperation* C. Fred Bergsten and Il SaKong, eds.
February 1995 ISBN 0-88132-213-X

International Debt Reexamined* William R. Cline
February 1995 ISBN 0-88132-083-8

American Trade Politics, 3d ed. I. M. Destler
April 1995 ISBN 0-88132-215-6

Managing Official Export Credits: The Quest for a Global Regime* John E. Ray
July 1995 ISBN 0-88132-207-5

Asia Pacific Fusion: Japan's Role in APEC* Yoichi Funabashi
October 1995 ISBN 0-88132-224-5

Korea-United States Cooperation in the New World Order* C. Fred Bergsten and Il SaKong, eds.
February 1996 ISBN 0-88132-226-1

Why Exports Really Matter!* ISBN 0-88132-221-0

Why Exports Matter More!* ISBN 0-88132-229-6 J. David Richardson and Karin Rindal
July 1995; February 1996

Global Corporations and National Governments Edward M. Graham
May 1996 ISBN 0-88132-111-7

Global Economic Leadership and the Group of Seven C. Fred Bergsten and C. Randall Henning
May 1996 ISBN 0-88132-218-0

The Trading System after the Uruguay Round* John Whalley and Colleen Hamilton
July 1996 ISBN 0-88132-131-1

Private Capital Flows to Emerging Markets after the Mexican Crisis* Guillermo A. Calvo, Morris Goldstein, and Eduard Hochreiter
September 1996 ISBN 0-88132-232-6

The Crawling Band as an Exchange Rate Regime: Lessons from Chile, Colombia, and Israel John Williamson
September 1996 ISBN 0-88132-231-8

Flying High: Liberalizing Civil Aviation in the Asia Pacific* Gary Clyde Hufbauer and Christopher Findlay
November 1996 ISBN 0-88132-227-X

Measuring the Costs of Visible Protection in Korea* Namdoo Kim
November 1996 ISBN 0-88132-236-9

The World Trading System: Challenges Ahead Jeffrey J. Schott
December 1996 ISBN 0-88132-235-0

Has Globalization Gone Too Far? Dani Rodrik
March 1997 ISBN paper 0-88132-241-5

Korea-United States Economic Relationship* C. Fred Bergsten and Il SaKong, eds.
March 1997 ISBN 0-88132-240-7

Summitry in the Americas: A Progress Report Richard E. Feinberg
April 1997 ISBN 0-88132-242-3

Corruption and the Global Economy Kimberly Ann Elliott
June 1997 ISBN 0-88132-233-4

Regional Trading Blocs in the World Economic System Jeffrey A. Frankel
October 1997 ISBN 0-88132-202-4

Sustaining the Asia Pacific Miracle: Environmental Protection and Economic Integration Andre Dua and Daniel C. Esty
October 1997 ISBN 0-88132-250-4

Trade and Income Distribution William R. Cline
November 1997 ISBN 0-88132-216-4

WORKS IN PROGRESS

**Australia, New Zealand,
and Papua New Guinea**
D. A. Information Services
648 Whitehorse Road
Mitcham, Victoria 3132, Australia
Tel: 61-3-9210-7777
Fax: 61-3-9210-7788
Email: service@dadirect.com.au
www.dadirect.com.au

India, Bangladesh, Nepal, and Sri Lanka
Viva Books Private Limited
Mr. Vinod Vasishtha
4737/23 Ansari Road
Daryaganj, New Delhi 110002
India
Tel: 91-11-4224-2200
Fax: 91-11-4224-2240
Email: viva@vivagroupindia.net
www.vivagroupindia.com

**Mexico, Central America, South America,
and Puerto Rico**
US PubRep, Inc.
311 Dean Drive
Rockville, MD 20851
Tel: 301-838-9276
Fax: 301-838-9278
Email: c.falk@ieee.org

Asia (*Brunei, Burma, Cambodia, China,
Hong Kong, Indonesia, Korea, Laos, Malaysia,
Philippines, Singapore, Taiwan, Thailand,
and Vietnam*)
East-West Export Books (EWEB)
University of Hawaii Press
2840 Kolowalu Street
Honolulu, Hawaii 96822-1888
Tel: 808-956-8830
Fax: 808-988-6052
Email: eweb@hawaii.edu

Canada
Renouf Bookstore
5369 Canotek Road, Unit 1
Ottawa, Ontario KlJ 9J3, Canada
Tel: 613-745-2665
Fax: 613-745-7660
www.renoufbooks.com

Japan
United Publishers Services Ltd.
1-32-5, Higashi-shinagawa
Shinagawa-ku, Tokyo 140-0002
Japan
Tel: 81-3-5479-7251
Fax: 81-3-5479-7307
Email: purchasing@ups.co.jp
*For trade accounts only. Individuals will find
Institute books in leading Tokyo bookstores.*

Middle East
MERIC
2 Bahgat Ali Street, El Masry Towers
Tower D, Apt. 24
Zamalek, Cairo
Egypt
Tel. 20-2-7633824
Fax: 20-2-7369355
Email: mahmoud_fouda@mericonline.com
www.mericonline.com

United Kingdom, Europe
(*including Russia and Turkey*)**, Africa,
and Israel**
The Eurospan Group
c/o Turpin Distribution
Pegasus Drive
Stratton Business Park
Biggleswade, Bedfordshire
SG18 8TQ
United Kingdom
Tel: 44 (0) 1767-604972
Fax: 44 (0) 1767-601640
Email: eurospan@turpin-distribution.com
www.eurospangroup.com/bookstore

**Visit our website at:
www.piie.com
E-mail orders to:
petersonmail@presswarehouse.com**